Meditations on Mystery

Other Publications by George Wolfe

The Spiritual Power of Nonviolence:
Interfaith Understanding for a Future
without War

Parallel Teaching in Hinduism and Christianity

Common Themes in the World's Great Religions

In the Shadow of the Sun: A Portrait of India

Versus Re-Verses

MEDITATIONS ON MYSTERY:

SCIENCE, PARADOX AND CONTEMPLATIVE SPIRITUALITY

George W. Wolfe

Dignity Press
World Dignity University Press

Published by:
Dignity Press,
16 Northview Court
Lake Oswego, OR 97035, USA

Book website:
www.dignitypress.org/meditations-on-mystery

All images in this book are in the public domain.
Cover art by Alfredo Marin-Carle

Printed on paper from environmentally managed forestry:
http://www.lightningsource.com/chainofcustody

ISBN 978-1-937570-49-1

Contents

In the Spirit of Zen

With patience, draw back the will
to follow the archer's path.

Take aim to penetrate the sky
with your melodies of silver
that warm the silence and still
the quivering breath.

Let go of becoming,
Ask without words,
Seek without longing,
Knock without sound.

Wade through streams of time
into the sanctuary of Being,
and there, wait for the arrow of insight
to slay all you think is real.

—GW

The Hermitage
Three Rivers, Michigan

Ever desireless, one can see the mystery,
Ever desiring, one can see the manifestations.
These two spring from the same source but differ in name;
This appears as darkness.
Darkness within darkness.
The gate of all mystery.

—Tao Te Ching,
Chapter 1

There is something beyond the mind which abides in silence within our mind. It is the supreme mystery beyond thought. Let one's mind and one's subtle body rest upon that and not rest on anything else.

—The Maitri Upanishad

Acknowledgments

I have always been fortunate to have friends willing to support my literary efforts. What began as a series of sermons I was invited to give at two local churches has taken shape in this book as I wrestled with my insights into science and spirituality.

Chapters one through four grew out of sermons I presented at the Unitarian Universalist Church in Muncie, Indiana. Chapter five first appeared as an article published in the interdisciplinary journal *Cross Currents*, and chapter six originated as a sermon I gave at the Unity Church in Anderson, Indiana.

I am sincerely grateful to all my colleagues who took time to read and critique earlier versions of the manuscript as I prepared it for publication. Special thanks must go to Rev. James Wolfe. As a world religions professor, his recommendations were invaluable as I developed and solidified my interfaith theology. Dr. Yeno Matuka also deserves special commendation. An author and former creative writing professor at Ball State University, the time he took out of his busy teaching schedule to critique my manuscript is much appreciated.

Sincere thanks must go to Bishop William E. Swing, Rev. John Denker and Dr. Jay Bagga for the time they took, not only to read the text but also to write endorsements that helped launch its publication. I am also grateful to Andrew Zimmerman Jones, co-author of *String Theory for Dummies* for advising me on the chapters that discuss aspects of Quantum Physics and for writing an endorsement. In addition, I want to thank my wife Susan Magrath for her thoughtful insights and encouragement, and also Sheryl Myers, Jayne Sample, David and Mary Lou Gotshall and other members of the Unity Church of Anderson, Indiana whose Sunday morning "Assets Class" discussed and critiqued my manuscript.

Finally, I am deeply grateful to Roger McConnell, director of America's Hometown Band, for letting me stay at his lakeside lodge so I could write without distractions, and to Alfredo Marin-Carle, an exceptionally gifted graphic artist in the Ball State University Department of Journalism, for designing the cover art.

Author's Note

This book examines religion in the context of mystery from an interfaith perspective. I have therefore chosen the designations CE (Common Era) and BCE (Before the Common Era) as a substitute for the traditional Western labels BC (Before Christ) and AD (Anno Domini). Unless otherwise indicated, all biblical references are from the Revised Standard Version and checked against the *Alfred Marshall Interlinear Greek-English New Testament* (Grand Rapids: Zondervan Publishing House, 1975). Some Bible verses have been edited to favor the use of inclusive language. Passages from the Qur'an, unless noted otherwise, are from *The Meaning of the Holy Qur'an* by Abdullah Yusuf Ali. With regards to Hindu, Buddhist and Taoist texts, multiple translations were often consulted.

Preface

We are living in a new age. No, not the Age of Aquarius as proclaimed by astrologers; not an Age of Enlightenment as heralded by the yogis. Rather this is the age of quantum physics, relativity, black holes, string theory, and the exponentially expanding universe. The universe of Isaac Newton is no more. Ours is a cosmos riddled with the bizarre and the mysterious.

In 2009, Stanford University physicist Leonard Susskind published his book *The Black Hole War: My Battle with Stephen Hawking to Make the World Safe for Quantum Mechanics*. In his own amusing style, Professor Susskind writes of the need for humans in the twenty-first century to "rewire" their brain's "neural networks" to accommodate the "new physics" which has provoked a paradigm shift that began in the early 1900s and is still continuing today.[1] This paradigm shift is the result of scientific discoveries in astrophysics, microbiology, holography and quantum field theory, and it is changing the way we perceive reality and humanity's relationship to the universe.

This book is the result of my personal effort to "rewire" my own "neural networks" to get a handle on the implications of these revolutionary discoveries. It is also my attempt to bring together believers and nonbelievers, and to reach people who fail to appreciate the rich mythology and wisdom that is found in ancient religious texts that continue to impact our world.

The concepts of paradox and uncertainty are inherent to modern physics. At the subatomic level, photons and other forms of "quanta" have both a particle and a wave nature. In our assessment of subatomic particle interactions, it is valid in certain cases to view particles as moving backwards in time. Electrons can be both localized and everywhere at the same time, and Werner Heisenberg discovered that uncertainty prevails when we try to determine the location and momentum (velocity) of subatomic particles. The more exact our knowledge of one of these variables, the less precise will be our knowledge of the other. In other words, there are some things, even in the physical universe, that we simply cannot know with certainty.

A primary difference between the scientist and the spiritual contemplative is that the contemplative can accept paradox and uncertainty as being in the nature of things. Paradoxes are to be embraced as a means of thinking more profoundly and deepening the conversation. The rational scientist, on the other hand, is only content when paradoxes are explained and mysteries solved. Indeed, there is a part of us that feels uncomfortable with uncertainty and wants to know all the answers. But the deeper we dig into the physical universe, the more questions present themselves and the more we are confronted with mystery.

In the process of "rewiring" my own "neural networks," I have looked at paradox and mystery by examining scripture, modern science (as opposed to classical Newtonian science) and the writings of religious mystics whose insights are remarkably compatible with reality as revealed by quantum mechanics, holography, and astrophysics. Understanding this compatibility brings about a reconciliation between modern science, contemplative spirituality and religious myth. In this reconciliation, a new awakening takes place whereby the conflict between reason and faith, and between subjectivity and objectivity, falls away. Albert Einstein's maxim, "Science without religion is lame; religion without science is blind," takes on new meaning. Without the insights and empathetic values that come to us through spirituality, science is reduced to a cold and dehumanizing worldview. It is my hope that all who read these pages will be left with a deeper appreciation of the emerging intersection of modern science and spirituality.

GW
Raccoon Lakeside Lodge
July 30, 2013

CHAPTER 1

Mystery, Paradox, and Two Kinds of Knowing

One must not think slightingly of the paradoxical ... for the paradox is the source of the thinker's passion, and the thinker without a paradox is like a lover without feeling: a paltry mediocrity.

—Søren Kierkegaard

I think I can safely say that nobody understands quantum mechanics. So do not take the lecture too seriously, feeling that you really have to understand in terms of some model, what I am going to describe, but just relax and enjoy it. I am going to tell you what nature behaves like. If you will simply admit that maybe she does behave like this, you will find her a delightful, entrancing thing.

—Richard Feynman

In the fall of 1980, I was teaching in Virginia at a university on the northern edge of a religiously conservative region of the United States known as the "Bible Belt." On September 28th, the television series Cosmos premiered on public television stations throughout the United States. The popular astronomer Carl Sagan, in collaboration with Ann Druyan and Steven Soter, wrote and narrated the thirteen part series.

As I listened to Professor Sagan introduce the first episode, the poetic language he was using to describe the universe he loved intrigued me. Sagan was a non-believer, yet he nevertheless was moved to invoke language that rang with mystical, even religious overtones.

Sagan spoke of the cosmos much like the sages have described God or the Ultimate Reality and how humanity descended into a state of unknowing. "Our contemplations of the cosmos stir us. There's a tingling in the spine, a catch in the voice, a faint sensation as if a distant memory of falling from a great height. We know we are approaching the grandest of mysteries."[1]

"The size and age of the cosmos," Sagan explains, "are beyond ordinary human understanding, lost somewhere between immensity and eternity"; the cosmos is "full beyond measure of elegant truths, of exquisite inter-relationships." And the cosmos, he says, is outside us but "also within us," as "we are made of star stuff," and as a result of our consciousness, "we are a way the cosmos can know itself"—words that sound more like the teachings of a Zen Buddhist philosopher.

In recent years, Father Thomas Keating, a Roman Catholic Priest and Trappist contemplative, has begun speaking of the Ultimate Reality using language that is remarkably similar to Sagan's. Keating speaks of the contemplative dimension of life as a means through which one comes to know the experience of "Ultimate Mystery."

> All who seek to participate in the experience of Ultimate Mystery—that is, the meaning of the Reality underlying the cosmos through the practice of religion, love of nature, science, art, dedicated service of others, deep friendship— are united in the same fundamental search. They can

remain in their own chosen path or religious tradition and still contribute to the unprecedented awakening of trans-cultural values that has begun to take place throughout the world. The most significant contribution they can make is to cultivate the experience of oneness with Ultimate Mystery, oneness with all other human beings, and oneness with the cosmos.[2]

How is it that an atheist and scientist like Sagan, and a Christian contemplative like Keating, find themselves using the same poetic phrases to describe the goal of their personal journeys of discovery? It is because in moments of personal reflection we seek deeper meaning, and in that act of reflection, we draw upon the mental faculties where poetic language and imagery are processed. These are the faculties of insight, intuition and realization that allow us to momentarily let go of logical and reductionist thinking so we can embrace an inexpressible wonder that enables us to appreciate the ineffable.

Carl Sagan (1934-1996)   Fr. Thomas Keating (b. 1923)
Two individuals, scientist and contemplative,
who appreciate the grandest of mysteries

Father Richard Rohr, author of *The Naked Now,* refers to this perception as "right-brain seeing and understanding," and as a "non-dualistic way of seeing the moment." As Rohr explains,

> Most of the major teachings of the great religions do not demand blind faith as much as new eyes. To the uninitiated, this always looks like blind faith, but it is in fact a different kind of light that allows—or creates—and even appreciates the shadows. Such light allows a compassionate, full, and patient reading of reality. It is often poets who see the truth and can communicate it best.[3]

Rohr further points out that a prominent feature of this new way of seeing is the awareness and appreciation of paradox.

> These new eyes have everything to do with seeing and thinking paradoxically—grasping the truth of something that seems a contradiction. ... What mystics have always known, great scientists now teach as well, and the church is trying to catch up after a long amnesia. ... Paradox is hidden and obvious, unless you have repressed one side of your very being.[4]

This "one side of your very being" is comprised of what customarily has been referred to as our "right-brain" mental faculties; i.e., those faculties that enable us to assess the moment in ways that are non-dual and holistic. They provide access to that subconscious level of the mind from which epiphanies dawn—those sudden realizations that reveal deeper meaning and transform the way we view the world.*

---

* The mental faculties that enable us to perceive in non-dual and holistic ways have routinely been associated with the right brain hemisphere. This

Appreciating Paradox and Allegory

Anyone who enjoys poetic language should enjoy paradox. If you are like me, you'll revel in the amusement paradoxes provide, and you'll become intrigued with trying to resolve them. At the very least, they provoke us into probing ideas with a heightened degree of focus and criticism.

In studying the sacred writings of the great religions, I have found, to my delight, that they are rich with paradox and irony. This is especially true with Taoist, Hindu, Buddhist, and Christian texts. Take for example the following passage from the Tao Te Ching.

> Yield and overcome;
> Bend and be straight;
> Empty and be full;
> Wear out and be new;
> Have little and gain.[5]

These lines express a philosophical view of life known as *value inversion* in which the values we normally see operating in the world are "inverted" or turned upside down. Christian scripture also contains examples of value inversion, as found in these well-known sayings attributed to Jesus:

> For everyone who exalts himself will be humbled, and he who humbles himself will be exalted. (Luke 14:11)

---

association, however, has been shown to be an over-simplification. Our brains function in ways that are much more complex. For this reason, throughout the remainder of this book, I avoid using the phrases "right-brained" and "left-brained" faculties.

> In the Kingdom of God many who are last shall be first,
> and the first, last. (Matt. 19:30)

> He who finds his life shall lose it. He who loses his life for
> my sake will find it. (Matt. 10:39)

Another example of paradox is found in the Katha Upanishad (ca. 500 BCE) which comes from the Hindu religious tradition and which includes some important themes found in the gospels. There we find the story of a boy named Nachiketa, "whose heart had received the truth taught in the scriptures," and whose father had given him over to die. The son comes to accept his destiny when he says, "Like corn, a man ripens and falls to the ground; like corn, he springs up again in his season."[6]* Nachiketa subsequently spends three nights in the house of the King of Death and afterwards receives three boons, the third of which is the secret of immortality. In the gospels, Jesus, who is to be given over to die, similarly recognizes his destiny when he says, "unless a grain of wheat falls into the earth and dies, it remains alone; but if it dies it bears much fruit" (John 12:24). He then spends three days in the tomb (the House of death) after which he is said to have overcome death and been raised to life eternal.

Both the story of Nachiketa spending three days in the house of the King of Death, and Christ spending three days in the tomb, convey a similar paradoxical message: it is through death that we gain immortality. In this context, death can be physical, as in the sacrificial death exemplified by the assassination of great nonviolent historical figures like Mahatma Gandhi and Martin Luther King Jr. who stood up against injustice. Their influence is still with us, even though they are gone. But death can also be expressed metaphori-

---

* In this passage, corn is not maize as we think of corn in Western countries. Rather, it is the kernel or seed of a grain such as rice, barley or wheat.

cally through symbols in allegories that refer to the death of the ego, and to the personal sacrifice of time and effort a person makes in life to serve others.

In the Zen Buddhist tradition, we find paradox expressed in riddles known as koans. Perhaps the most well-known koan is the question, "What is the sound of one hand clapping?"* Another one of my favorite koans captures the dilemma of using words to express Ultimate Reality: "It cannot be expressed in words, yet, it cannot be expressed without words." The art of writing poetry is inherently paradoxical, because, in the process of writing, the poet is *using words* to evoke feelings that *cannot be expressed in words*.

I enjoy composing modern koans of my own using the language of science and philosophy. Consider, the following examples:

> What is the nature of that question, the answer to which can only be heard in the silence that precedes its asking?

> If the Big Bang occurred 14 billion years ago and no one was around to hear it, did it make a sound?

> Have you discovered who you were before you had a name?

Many Jewish Hasidic tales also apply the concept of value inversion. A favorite Hasidic story of mine tells of a rabbi who was seated along the side of a street quietly watching people pass by. Soon an older man walks by at a hurried pace, clearly burdened and under stress by the load of goods he is carrying. Seeing his distress, the rabbi asks him: "Sir, what are you doing?"

The man, looking at the rabbi with some contempt, replies, "I'm pursuing my livelihood!"

---

* For an explanation of a possible answer to this koan, see the footnote on the last page of chapter 5.

The rabbi responds: "How do you know it is out in front of you? Perhaps it is behind you, and all you need to do is be still." The rabbi in this story may be alluding to Psalm 46:10 which says, "Be still, and know that I am God." Listen to your Divine inner voice so your livelihood can catch up with you!

Oftentimes, people miss the humor inherent to paradoxical stories found in religious texts. The story in the Bible of Balaam and his stubborn donkey is a good example.

An Israelite named Balaam arose one morning to travel with the princes of Moab. But God had positioned an angel with a drawn sword to stand in his way. The angel was seen by the donkey, but not by Balaam. The donkey refused to pass by the angel, frustrating Balaam and causing him to strike the donkey. This happened three times until God caused the donkey to speak. Then Balaam's "eyes were opened" so that he could see the angel blocking his path (Numbers 22:21–30). I can't help but chuckle at the paradoxical humor in this story, where the truth is revealed to the hero of the story by a jackass!

The author of a New Testament epistle attributed to the apostle Peter appears to be aware of this paradox when he writes, "A dumb ass spoke to Balaam with a human voice and restrained the prophet's madness" (2 Peter 2:16).

Like many Zen and Taoist tales, the story teaches us not to make dismissive assumptions. We should never overlook the possible significance of anything or any creature, no matter how lowly. Insight can often come to us through the simplest and most mundane sources.

One of the most puzzling examples of paradox in the Christian scriptures is found at the end of the ninth chapter of the Gospel of John after Jesus heals a man who was born blind. The entire chapter is devoted to demonstrating how the process of intellectual inquiry used by the religious leaders in the synagogue, which relies heavily on logical argument and the verbal testimony of witnesses, is inadequate when applied to discerning the truth. Witnesses, including the man who was healed, are called upon to give their personal account of what happened. How is it that a wandering teacher healed someone on the Sabbath who had been blind from birth? The scene described is one of confusion as the religious leaders try to evaluate the testimony and align it with their understanding of the Mosaic Law.

> The Pharisees again asked him how he had received his sight. And he said to them, "He put clay on my eyes, and I washed, and I see." Some of the Pharisees said, "This man is not from God, for he does not keep the Sabbath." But others said, "How can a man who is a sinner, do such signs?" There was a division among them. (John 9:15, 16)

This pursuit for truth is finally abandoned leaving Jesus in conversation with the man he healed. Jesus then makes the following koan-like paradoxical statement, "I came into the world so that those who do not see may see, and those who see may be made blind" (John 9:39–41). Some of the Pharisees who remained behind overheard the conversation and said, "Are we also blind?" to which Jesus replied, "If you were blind, you would have no guilt; but now that you say 'We see,' your guilt remains" (John 9:40, 41). Herein lies a possible clue for deciphering Jesus' paradoxical statement. "Seeing" in this passage is a metaphor for those who think they know, think they understand, but who are actually lacking in knowledge because they are relying on their intellect. They are unable to perceive with their inner non-dualistic "sight" through which one can truly see.

Jesus may also be alluding to the Garden of Eden myth. When Adam and Eve disobeyed God's commandment and ate the fruit from the tree of knowledge of good and evil, their "eyes were opened" so they would know good and evil (Gen. 3: 5, 7). They also saw that they were naked, which is a symbol of being exposed and vulnerable. Knowing good and evil implies that a person is in the habit of judging others in simplistic, dualist ways. The Pharisees were passing judgment on the events that had taken place, and on the man who was born blind. But Jesus was speaking of a knowledge that can only be perceived from the state of innocence in which Adam and Eve lived prior to their disobedience. If we can return to this nonjudgmental condition of innocence where we can stand in our nakedness, we can know the truth that transcends the domain of legalistic, intellectual inquiry. Only then can we appreciate the mystery and the deeper miracle that had actually taken place with the man born blind.*

Oftentimes, a paradoxical meaning is hidden within a narrative that is being dramatized as an historical event. A story about the apostle Paul in the New Testament book of Acts illustrates this idea of hidden paradox.

Paul and his followers had been arrested and were shackled in a prison cell. As they sat in prison, they began singing hymns when a earthquake struck, shaking the prison's foundation, jarring open the cell doors and releasing them from their shackles. The jailer, who had been instructed to guard them with his life, drew a sword to kill himself. But Paul and his followers remained in their cell, and called to him, telling him to wait as they were still there and had not fled. The jailer then entered the cell, and realizing that

---

* The myth of Adam and Eve in the Garden of Eden can also be understood as an ancient child-development theory. Every child is born in a state of innocence. Then, as they approach two years of age, they become aware of right and wrong, good and evil, and must be taught rules, or a "law" to live by. Soon thereafter, children, like Adam and Eve, become aware of their nudity, and out of embarrassment, no longer wish to be seen naked. Adam and Eve, not knowing that they were naked prior to their transgression, is a metaphor for living in a nonjudgmental condition of innocence, which is a precondition for knowledge that is free from prejudice.

Paul was not afraid, bowed before him and asked how he could be saved from his predicament as a jailer, and also from death itself (see Acts 16:19–30).

The paradox in this story reveals that the "prison" Paul and his followers were shackled in is a metaphor for circumstances that keep us from living a life in a state of spiritual freedom. The person in this story who was actually in prison was the jailer because he was bound to the punishment of death if Paul had escaped. But the apostle and his followers, who remained in their cell despite the fact that the doors were ajar and their shackles loosened, were spiritually liberated. They had nothing to escape from. The prison, therefore, is actually within us, and freedom is dependent on our ability to live a life unfettered by materialistic concerns and political trappings.

To "see" the spiritual messages in paradoxical koans and stories, one needs to be awakened to an awareness that can depart from a literal, historical view and embrace metaphor and allegory. A person must adopt a language that is somewhat removed from the world in which we conduct our mundane, commercial and political affairs. This is not to say there is no room for material generosity and political involvement, only that our actions become inspired and powered by metaphor and symbolic language. The Rev. Dr. Martin Luther King Jr. used such language in his inspirational "I have a dream" speech delivered in 1963 in front of the Lincoln Memorial.

In an online video, physicist Richard Feynman refers to ancient creation myths as "theories," the implication being that these ancient legends have been replaced by more informed, research-based explanations offered by science. That ancient creation myths are theories is a common misconception held by many atheists, and also by many believers. A theory grows out of a reasoned assessment of observed events and generates a hypothesis that hopefully can one day be tested. Myths and legends are forms of storytelling. They are meant to awaken us to paradox and mystery and be a catalyst for philosophical discussion.

Ancient creation stories found in religious scripture are not theories. Rather, they are a genre of literature—myths that harbor great symbolic meaning. They were written by poets, not scientists. They are intended to inspire people to think deeply about the origins of the cosmos, human existence, the relationship humans are to have with one another, the natural world, and the incomprehensible power that gave rise to the unfolding space-time continuum we call the universe.

This view is supported by the fact that there are actually two creation stories in the book of Genesis that appear to contradict each other. The first story is in Genesis, Chapter 1, while the second is in Chapter 2. It is believed the story told in Genesis 2 was actually written earlier. In Chapter 1, Adam, the prototypical man, is created last. In Chapter 2, he is created first, after which he gives names to all things that are created (Gen.: 2:20). The subject of relationship is explored between Adam and his mate, Eve, and between the first couple and their creator.

In my book *The Spiritual Power of Nonviolence: Interfaith Understanding for a Future without War*, I point out that both of these biblical creation myths are nonviolent. It is in Genesis, Chapter 4, when Adam's son Cain kills his brother Abel, that violence is recognized as becoming part of the human experience.

These two ancient myths were meant to inspire discussion between Rabbis and their disciples, ultimately resulting in dialogs that led to the Jewish commentaries known as the Talmud. Perhaps these contradictory tales were used to generate dialog on the enduring question: "To what extent can creation exist without human consciousness, without us being here to experience it, name it and give it reality?"

That ancient creation stories should be viewed as allegorical works of literature rather than theories is complicated by the fact that the literary style of ancient writers often merged myth and history.

Homer's *Illiad*, for example, set the Trojan War around such characters as Achilles, whose mother had dipped him in the river Styx. This made him invulnerable as a warrior except for his heel, which his mother held on to while immersing him in the river. The name Achilles refers to the "grief of the people," an appropriate image that relates to the tragedy of war. And by including Achilles, Homer's dramatization of history also alludes to a myth that warns us of a significant truth; that is, no matter how powerful and influential we may become, there is always a weakness somewhere that makes us vulnerable and has the potential to bring about our downfall.

Jewish writers who wrote much of the Bible were exceptionally good at integrating myth and history and did so in such a convincing manner that for many people, it is difficult to determine where history leaves off and myth begins.

For example, the history of the Israelites, as told in the book of Exodus, begins with the Israelites as slaves in Egypt. Upon their escape, they migrate from Egypt through the desert, eventually settling in the land of Canaan, which they believe to be their Promised Land. But included in this history is the story of God having Moses stretch out his arms to part the Red Sea. The Israelites pass through on dry land, after which the waters return to destroy the pursuing Egyptian army (Exodus 14:15–29). Myth or history? Allegorically, the separation of the waters can be viewed as a birth metaphor intended to symbolize the birthing of a new nation.* It also teaches that when we confront an insurmountable obstacle, if our intentions are pure, a force far greater than ourselves will help us endure and allow us to pass through.

---

*   Before a woman gives birth, her water breaks, signaling the beginning of labor.

Earlier in Exodus, when Moses questions whether his people would believe him, God commands him to cast the rod he was carrying onto the ground, whereupon it turns into a serpent, only to become a rod again when Moses picks it up (Exodus 4:1–5). An allegorical interpretation suggests this mythological embellishment testifies to the conquering power of God's wisdom over evil, the serpent intended as a symbol for temptation and deception as it was so used in the Garden of Eden myth.*

Ancient literary masters created religiously inspired histories and brought forth a language infused with poetic beauty, vision, and the richness of symbolism. It is a language that is purposefully ambiguous so as to allow for multiple interpretations. This is not the language of science. Rather, it is the language of scripture, the language of psalms, the language of paradox, and the language of a literary style that weaves together myth and history. And as explained by Fr. Richard Rohr, an important purpose of religion is to "give us that eye for paradox and mystery."[7]

---

* As an allegory, the story of the Exodus provided inspiration for African slaves in the United States, images of which are expressed often in Negro spirituals. The Southern slaveholder became the pharaoh; freedom in the north, the Promised Land; and Harriet Tubman, who covertly led many slaves to freedom using the safe houses of the Underground Railroad, became known as the black Moses. Mystics view the story of the Exodus as an allegorical journey to spiritual enlightenment. The slavery of the Israelites is a metaphor for being in bondage to ignorance. To be lost in the wilderness symbolizes the personal quest to free oneself from repetitive negative habits (i.e., a person who is lost tends to walk in circles or make the same mistakes in life over and over). Entering the Promised Land represents the liberation of the spirit which is the culmination of the path to enlightenment.

Two Ways to Define Mystery

We tend to lump all mysteries together into one category, but there are actually two kinds of mystery. The first kind deals with phenomena that either cannot be known or are not yet known. Have microbial life forms ever existed on Mars? How and for what reason were the giant statues, or *moai*, on Easter Island carved, moved and set in place? Many people may speculate, but no one as yet can answer these questions with certainty. Indeed, their answers may never be available to us. Such questions fall into this first category of mystery. This is the way a scientist, a researcher, or an investigative reporter would define a mystery.

The second kind asserts that a mystery is something that *is* known, *can* be experienced, *can* be appreciated, but when it is experienced, one recognizes there is something about it that is incomprehensible. One has encountered a phenomenon that is beyond the human mind to fully grasp, the meaning of which words are inadequate to express. We may have this reaction when we ponder how, prior to the "Big Bang" that gave rise to the universe, time and space were nonexistent, merged into a "singularity," or when we see deep space photos from the Hubble Space Telescope peering 14 billion years back in time to reveal innumerable galaxies, each containing billions of stars. Or we may respond with awe and wonder as I did when, in California, I sauntered amidst the giant sequoia trees in the upper Sierra. Their majesty overwhelms, in much the same way as we can be deeply moved by an exceptionally beautiful or profound work of art. This experience of the incomprehensible is the way a spiritual contemplative would define mystery.

The point Thomas Keating raises, however, that we "seek to participate in the experience of Ultimate Mystery," even to "cultivate the experience of oneness with Ultimate Mystery,"[8] takes our inquiry beyond the scientific realm and into the domain of spirituality.

While the concept of "spirit" may seem vague, indefinable and problematic to a scientist, to the artist it is a very tangible, experiential phenomenon. The Italian expression *con spirito*, (i.e. "with spirit"), is a common marking in musical scores.

Spirit is the energy that animates and brings an artwork to life. It is what inspires, generates passion and makes possible an intense mental focus. Spirit also gives a person clarity of mind and a determined will.

To my students, I explain spirit as being comparable to the concept of "chi" in Chinese Taoist philosophy. While our outer physical strength fades as we grow old, chi is the inner strength that can actually grow stronger as one ages. It is chi that enables a person to see their way through the trials of life and acquire great social influence that can endure well beyond death.

In ancient languages such as Chinese, Greek, Hebrew and Arabic, the word for spirit is also associated with breath.* This linguistic association implies a life-force that is very much a part of the performing artist's concept of what makes any artistic performance exceptional. Unfortunately, in English and other modern languages, there are two quite different words for spirit and breath, and thus this association has been lost to the point that many people view spirit as an idea that is obsolete. Such is not the case, however, for those who engage in a regular spiritual practice that gives one direct access to inner strength.

An awakened spiritual energy instills within us a sense of wholeness and a higher, more inclusive level of awareness whereby we experience the ineffable and recognize the whole as greater than the sum of its parts. One becomes a visionary with a positive sense

---

* Examples of words for spirit in ancient languages that also refer to or imply the concept of breath are as follows: Arabic—ruh, Hebrew—ruach, Chinese—chi, Greek—pneuma. In the Gospel of John, Ch. 20 verse 22, it says that Jesus "breathed" on his disciples and said: "Receive the Holy Spirit" (pneuma).

of purpose and the power to manifest one's vision. The spirit is that force which enables us to exceed our expectations, to experience what psychologist Abraham Maslow called the peak experience. Moreover, it is the spirit that distinguishes the creative self-modifying intelligence in humans from the programmed artificial intelligence of machines.

Skeptics say that inspired states of mind and peak experiences can be explained by random chance and biochemical changes in the body, but the fact is they can't entirely. Anyone who has been deeply in love with someone or something knows that lasting love and commitment are more than hormones. Anyone who has had a peak experience, where they lifted an entire team or audience and performed well beyond expectations, knows that spirit is intimately connected with both individual and collective will power. It is focus and determination, mind over matter so to speak, made possible by the human spirit, that makes these transforming experiences possible.

We see this often in the performing arts, athletics and in social activists like Alice Paul, Rev. Dr. Martin Luther King Jr. and Lech Wałęsa who mustered up the courage to stand against injustice.

Live your life "con spirito," with spirit; that is what will make it dynamic, meaningful, and inspiring to others. That is what grants us our measure of immortality.

But can a person develop, or sense, a personal relationship with the Ultimate Mystery? Can we, in some way, actually *know* Ultimate Mystery? To answer these questions, we must realize that there are two distinctly different kinds of knowing.

The English language is confusing when it comes to defining what it means *to know* because in English, there is only one word for the verb "to know." There are other languages that have two words for knowing. In French for example, if you are speaking about knowing a piece of information, such as a telephone number, or knowing how to perform a task or a skill, such as dialing the phone number, a person would use the verb "savoir." But if you are talking about knowing a person, or being familiar with something or someone, you would use the verb "connaître."

Why? Because knowing a person or being deeply familiar with someone, is much different than knowing a piece of information, or how something is done. Once you know the phone number you are asking for, your knowledge with regard to that piece of information is complete. But when it comes to knowing a *person*, you never really do know them completely. A person has, or at least should have, the depth of mind that enables them to change or respond unexpectedly. He or she is still growing, evolving and developing psychologically. It is this second kind of knowing that enables you to pick out the perfect gift for your spouse. It is also this second kind of knowing that causes one to break into tears and mourn when your loved one dies. And it is through this second kind of knowing that a person can develop a personal relationship with Ultimate Mystery.

Relationship is deepened and made personal through our mental faculties that give us access to the affective or aesthetic domains of experience. We accomplish this when we gain a deep appreciation of an artist, poet, philosopher, actor or musician. We get to know that person, not as a famous personality that we know superficially, but as a person we know inwardly through close association. This experience requires us to be open and receptive to our feelings and to how we are moved by the aesthetic experience. And this openness is a form of surrender, which is a means of getting beyond the ego. To have a personal relationship with Ultimate Mystery requires this form of surrender.

Spiritual contemplatives are people who have experienced Ultimate Mystery and recognize the importance and legitimacy of the ineffable in one's life. They realize the Ultimate Mystery is a living presence in a way similar to experiencing an important and thoughtful person as having an ongoing influence in one's life, even though that person may not be physically present. Spiritual contemplatives have had at least momentary experiences of becoming one with Ultimate Mystery, either through meditation or through a ritual that leads a person into that realm of experience. They believe it is possible to know Ultimate Mystery in a way analogous to how an individual seeks to know another person, through an ongoing process of study and reflection that deepens the relationship.

From this kind of knowing, we come to marvel at the illusory nature of time, space, objectivity and the material realm we experience, how it is that the source of creation and the universe in which we live cannot be fully comprehended, and how consciousness, which is prerequisite for human experience and for understanding the cosmos, must coexist with the material universe.* This vision of reality is no longer the mere fantasy of mystics. It is a viewpoint that is valid according to what we now know from quantum physics. As Larry Dossey explains in his book *Space, Time and Medicine*:

> No feature of quantum physics is more revolutionary than its acknowledgement of the subjective aspects of the world. The classical [Newtonian] view held the world to be totally objective. It was "out there," depending in no way for human conscious activity to bring it into being. ... In the modern view, however ... human consciousness participates in the edition of the reality that meets our eye. In fact, without an observer, the concept of "reality" simply has no currency. ... Without the participation of an observer, what we refer to as reality simply does not unfold. Thus the strictly objective status of the physical world has been transcended in the new view, and replaced

---

*   The physical universe as an illusion will be discussed in more detail in chapters 2 and 6.

by a version of reality which attributes central importance to human consciousness.[9]

That consciousness is perhaps best expressed in Hindu scripture as "that which cannot be seen by the eye, but by which the eye sees … that which cannot be heard by the ear but by which the ear hears … that which cannot be comprehended by the mind, but by which the mind comprehends."[10]

CHAPTER 2

The Spirituality of Spring

The most beautiful and deepest experience a man can have is the sense of the mysterious. It is the underlying principle of religion as well as all serious endeavor in art and science. He who never had this experience seems to me, if not dead, then at least blind. To sense that behind anything that can be experienced there is a something that our mind cannot grasp and whose beauty and sublimity reaches [sic] us only indirectly and as a feeble reflection, this is religiousness. In this sense I am religious. To me it suffices to wonder at these secrets and to attempt humbly to grasp with my mind a mere image of the lofty structure of all that there is.

—Albert Einstein

How wonderful that we have met with a paradox. Now we have some hope of making progress.

—Niels Bohr

Reverend Leishman served for several years in the Presbyterian Church I attended as a boy in Corry, Pennsylvania. One stunning fall Sunday, many of the pews in the sanctuary were empty. I remember well his words as he reconciled himself with the poor attendance: "There are two things you can't fight in this world," he said. "City hall and the autumn leaves."

His words resonate in me now like a Biblical proverb. Ever since I moved to Indiana, I have come to realize what a treasure the fall season is. In the best of years, the palette of colors in mid-October is spectacular. Perhaps it is because I am of the age where I identify with the season of decline, but each year now I literally crave the colors. The autumn beauty is like a tonic I long to imbibe my mind in each year, and I enjoy drinking in the colors as much as the apple cider that is pressed in the old-fashioned cider mills.

This is the time of year I plan a healthy hike at Mounds State Park near Anderson, Indiana. After relocating in the neighboring city of Muncie in 1982, I became fascinated with the Native American earthworks in the park. There are said to be 10 mounds within the park's borders, the most impressive being the Great Circle Mound. From the visitor's center, a quarter mile hike through a comforting forest that crosses a chiseling stream takes one to this sizeable earthwork. If a person listens deeply, the mind will resonate with the rituals of shamans whose songs sanctified this land. One cannot help but feel the presence of a people who inscribed their immortal mark in a forest that still harbors their heritage and the Great Spirit they revered. It is the voice of this Spirit that I sought to express in the following poem.

> I am the forgotten One, hidden beneath currents of
> thought and mood, wrapped in a blanket of solitude.
> I am That to which forest streams pray without ceasing
> while adorned with color and passing leaves.
>
> I speak the language of the river, whose syllables
> rhyme with the phases of the moon, whose
> rapids are the songs of shamans trying
> endlessly to heal this world.

They wash hate from the shores of humanity, and cast aside
the silt of history from which sprouts the rice of renewal.
I am the center, the circle is my dream. Remember as you
listen for tribal voices calling you to My sacred home.

In the early 1980s, researchers at Ball State University discovered
that the placement of several of the mounds in the park aligns with
either the sunrise or sunset on the winter and summer solstice. A
group of local Native Americans gather at the Great Mound for each
solstice, and also at the time of the vernal and autumnal equinox.
Seeking to keep alive an ancient tradition, they perform an authentic
ritual marking the beginning of each new season.

Since ancient times, humans have been intrigued by such celestial
events. The spring equinox is especially significant to earth-centered
religions, but it is also important to members of the Baha'i faith, as
Naw-Ruz, the Baha'i New Year, falls on the twenty-first of March. In
addition to seasonal markers, there is great public interest whenever
there occurs a lunar or solar eclipse, a rare conjunction of planets,
the appearance of a comet, or the rather farfetched notion that the
world was to end on December 21st, 2012, when the sun aligned
itself with the center of our galaxy.

I have come to believe that this fascination with celestial alignments expresses a deeply rooted subconscious need. As humans we
seek to align ourselves with life, organizing our daily routines to
be in synchrony with the rhythms of nature. We long for harmony
in our social lives and with the natural world. Celestial alignments
are a metaphor for this fundamental human need. They provide us
with reference points that help us make sense out of a world that is
filled with events that seem random and meaningless.

Thousands of years ago, these alignments were a mystery that
held great significance for our ancestors. Out of such observa-
tions emerged the pseudoscience of astrology. But today, thanks
to advances in astronomy, the movements of the sun, moon and

stars, and their alignment with our planet, are understood. They are predictable and no longer seen as mysterious.

Sometime ago I attended a funeral at which a Roman Catholic priest was officiating. During his sermon, he spoke of the resurrection of Christ as a mystery.

"People ask me," he said, "'How do you explain it?' And my answer is, 'You can't explain it. It's a mystery.'"

When I heard this, it was not a statement I initially could accept. It was as if he had resigned himself to never knowing, refusing to engage in the process of inquiry or questioning the Church's "party line." And it seemed at the time to be quite contrary to what Jesus himself taught when he warned against blind faith, describing so many of the spiritual leaders of his day as the "blind leading the blind." The term "faith," is more correctly understood as trust, not blind acceptance. We have faith in ideas, in people and relationships that we trust. And trust can only be truly gained through experience and by questioning and thinking deeply.

In the spring of 2011, I spoke on several panels at the International Conference of World Affairs in Boulder, Colorado. The topic for one of the panel discussions was "Defining Faith." Knowing that I was addressing a skeptical audience, I chose to explain the relationship between faith and reason using the metaphor of marriage.

When a couple decides to make a life-long commitment, that decision, either consciously or unconsciously, is based on both faith (trust) and reason. No matter how well you know the person you are about to marry, you cannot know your future spouse well enough to predict with certainty, what they will be like 10 or 20 years hence. To make that kind of a long term commitment requires faith, but such faith is not devoid of reason. One must apply reason to assess the integrity and sincerity of your potential spouse. That assessment is an evaluation based on our experience with that person and knowing them on a deep level. One then takes what is called in religious circles a "leap of faith." We leap into a realm of future, and to some degree unknown, possibilities. We love what we know about the person we are about to marry, but we are left to trust what we do not know about them, and about what the future holds. It is a process I call *informed surrendering*.

The decision to marry someone shows there is no contradiction between faith and reason. Reason requires intellect; faith requires insight. A life of faith is a life of informed surrendering, a blending of predictability with uncertainty and trust.

Regardless whether a person is a believer or nonbeliever, it becomes clear that it is impossible to live without some degree of faith. All thoughtful, long-term decisions must incorporate both faith and reason in order to make judgments that are meaningful and well informed. Applied together, faith and reason complement each other and result in a perspective that is both informed and wise.

Knowledge Revealed from Within

During its first 100 years, Christianity was one of several "mystery religions" of its day. Many of its followers in the first few centuries after the crucifixion of Jesus were Gnostic Christians. In Gnosticism, however, mystery was more akin to knowledge. The Greek word *Gnosis*, from which Gnostic is derived, means knowledge. But this is not empirical, scientific knowledge. Rather, it is knowledge gained through insight. It is truth that is revealed from within rather than taken in from without.

In 325 CE, Constantine, who was then the sole emperor of the Roman Empire, called a conference of church leaders to meet in the city of Nicaea. At what became known as the Council of Nicaea, those leaders in attendance condemned Gnosticism as a heresy.

Rather than encourage the believers to be led by their insights, a rigid dogma was imposed to reign in would-be prophets and visionaries. This occurred in spite of the fact that the apostle Paul's conversion experience on the road to Damascus fits well within the framework of the Gnostic experience.

Despite the repression of Gnosticism by the church, ideas dear to the Gnostics are found in the four gospels that are part of the Christian Canon. Perhaps most familiar is the concept of epiphany.

The season of epiphany in the church recalls the allegorical journey of the Magi, or wise men from the east, to visit the Christ child. They were following a "star," which symbolizes a light or a guide that is external or outside oneself. This external knowledge is shown to be incomplete, because when the Magi arrive in Judea, they have to visit King Herod and ask where they could find the infant Jesus. But once they found the Christ child, which represents the light of knowledge within us, they could have an epiphany. This epiphany came to them in a dream, instructing them to change course and venture home without returning to tell Herod of the child's whereabouts. Like the Magi who were prompted to take a different path homeward, epiphanies, especially those that are profound, often result in a change of direction in our life's journey.

The word epiphany is defined as "a sudden realization of truth." The experience of having an epiphany usually dawns as an "ah ha" experience that is more accurately described as an inner awakening, taking us to deeper levels of perception. An answer dawns from deep within the mind, emerging from the darkness of the subconscious, as if to be born from the womb of mystery. Knowledge is revealed from within, and a spiritual teacher is someone who knows how to trigger this type of awakening in a disciple.

Unfortunately, as the early church leaders imposed their rigid dogma, the story of the Magi was reduced to a mere historical event, and the concept of epiphany as an inner experience was minimized and even forgotten.

Reviving the experience of epiphany leads us into the fascinating study of symbolism and allegorical meaning in scripture, and not just in Christian texts, but in Hindu, Buddhist, Jewish and Islamic writings as well. Once we can look beyond the historical context of religion, we discover deeper possibilities of interpretation. This pursuit then becomes an exercise in inner growth and understanding, much like koans are used by Zen Masters to awaken their disciples.

Historical accuracy and authenticity are of lesser importance when contrasted with the allegorical meaning of the events depicted in the Bible. Even within Christian scripture, the apostle Paul delves into symbolic meaning. In his letter to the Galatians, for example, Paul refers to Abraham's two sons, one born to Abraham's wife Sarah, and the other to Hagar, his slave woman. He then proceeds to interpret this story as an allegory, "Behold, I show you an allegory" (see Gal. 4:22–26).

Careful examination reveals that the gospels are written more like a drama than as an historical account, suggesting much of the gospel narrative is intended to have allegorical meaning as well as historical significance. Take for example the scene of Jesus before Pontius Pilate in the Gospel of John.

After Jesus is humiliated with a mock royal robe and a crown of thorns, Pilate takes Jesus aside into his quarters. In a private conversation, he asks a few questions about whether or not Jesus is really a king. Jesus answers, "My kingship is not of this world," then later in the dialog adds, "I have come into the world, to bear witness to the truth." Pilate then responds with the enduring philosophical question: "What is truth?" (John 18:36–38). The conversation then abruptly ends, the scene suddenly changes, and the drama of Christ's Passion continues.

How then was this conversation recorded? There was no one else present in the room with Pilate and Jesus. This dialog was constructed to enhance the drama, and provoke the reader into thinking deeply about the final question Pilate asked. I also suspect the question, "What is truth," was included to show, among other things, that Pilate was ignorant of the truth, lest he would not have had to ask the question.

Early in the gospels, Jesus is depicted as clearing the temple in Jerusalem of the moneychangers (John 2:14–21). Much has been made by scholars of the timing of Jesus' righteous rage and the probable response of the Romans to this disruptive action. Immediately afterwards, in the Gospel of John, Jesus responds to questions by referring to the temple as a metaphor for his body: "Destroy this temple, and in three days I will raise it up" (John 2:19–21). His words suggest there is an allegorical meaning to this story that applies to us all, regardless of our religious persuasion. In this context, the temple becomes the temple of the body. The moneychangers symbolize our own inner greed and selfishness. The story challenges us to call upon our higher moral nature, symbolized by the Christ figure, to rid our bodily temple of our shortsighted selfish desires (i.e., the moneychangers).

One way this is accomplished is by practicing a form of meditation or reflective prayer that settles the mind into a condition of inner contentment, the state of non-desire. Every time I sit to meditate, I purge my bodily temple of the moneychangers that dwell within me.

In addition to allegory, mystery is also contained in symbols and parables. As a young adult, I never thought to question the description of the Promised Land as a "land flowing with milk and honey" (Exodus 3:8; 13:5; 33:3). Eventually I snapped out of my complacency enough to ask, "Why milk and honey?" It seemed quite strange to describe a land with such a peculiar phrase. This was a mystery for me, but one that I sought to find an explanation for, rather than blindly accept.

Years later, during my first trip to India, I purchased an anthology of the Rig Veda. Within its many hymns I discovered that milk and honey were ancient fertility symbols. Honey symbolized wealth because of its golden color and sumptuous taste, and milk represented rain as, poetically speaking, it was said that the rain was as if "milked" from the clouds.[1] Now the phrase "a land flowing with milk and honey" began to make sense, as it would be fitting to describe a Promised Land using fertility symbols.

In 2003, I mentioned this symbolism to a rabbi I studied with briefly in New York City named Joseph Gelberman. Speaking in a Yiddish accent, he responded with the following anecdote.

"About 4000 years ago, when the Israelites were in the wilderness, God said to them, 'Ok, I will give you a land to live on. And I will give you a choice. You can have a land flowing with milk and honey, or a land flowing with oil. Which would you like?' "

"Unfortunately," the rabbi quipped, "we chose the milk and honey."

One of the more bewildering mysteries in the gospels is the story of Jesus cursing the fig tree (Matt. 21:20). When passing by a fig tree with his disciples, he noticed the tree was not bearing fruit. This was to be expected, since the tree was not in season. But Jesus cursed the tree anyway for not being productive.

It turns out the seasons have been used since ancient times as a metaphor for the four stages of life, these being youth symbolized by spring, middle-age symbolized by summer, retirement which is represented by autumn, and old age being the season of winter. It is in the summer of life that a person is to "bear fruit," entering into a committed relationship, advancing one's career, and accumulating wealth to provide for one's dependents. Once we enter the fall season of life, we are, as if, "out of season." Our opportunities for advancement (bearing fruit) begin to wane. But Jesus is telling us we must not be like the fruitless fig tree. Rather, we must find new ways to contribute to society and "bear fruit," lest we be cursed with cynicism and, in our frustration, see the human condition as hopeless.

I have seen this cynicism overtake several of my colleagues, many of whom are retired and feel they have lost their relevance and their ability to have an impact on peoples' lives.

This parable has had great meaning for me as I enter retirement and lose my edge as a professional musician. Younger and more ambitious faculty associates are waiting in the wings to fill my niche.

To avoid the curse of cynicism, we must continue to serve humanity through whatever gifts we have been given or have developed over the course of our life.

These examples show how the mysteries contained in parables, symbolism, and allegory become an exercise in thinking deeply and awakening our faculties of insight and realization.

I must emphasize, however, that any particular interpretation of scripture I offer in this book is simply one of several possibilities. These are interpretations that have been meaningful in my own life journey. The beauty of personal insight is that new interpretations arise as our journey through life unfolds and that other sojourners can offer their own unique and personal insights. The sages' use of symbolism, poetic imagery and paradoxical language makes possible multiple interpretations. Our role is to ponder, not to judge.

Awakening as an Interfaith Experience

When my daughter Esther was four years old, she rescued a rose bud that was attached to a broken stem. She brought it into our house where I trimmed off the end. We then set the stem in a vase and placed the rose bud on a sunlit windowsill in her bedroom.

The next morning Esther came running out of her room, her face bright with astonishment.

"Daddy, Daddy!" she exclaimed. "You know that rose bud we put in my room yesterday? When I woke up this morning, IT HAD BLOOMED!"

Like a proud father, I was delighted, as any dad would be, to hear her infectious enthusiasm. She had come to me like someone who had just seen a miracle. Knowing the science behind the phenomenon she had witnessed, I responded with my own artificial amazement, not wanting to diminish the surprise that had suddenly awakened her to one of the marvels of nature. I soon realized that I too had been awakened, not by the blooming rose bud, but by my daughter's spirit of wonder. It then occurred to me that I had been taking this and other small miracles for granted. To a significant degree, I had lost my innocence and my ability to perceive the world through a child's eyes. I had become blind in that I had been dismissing the validity of an aesthetic experience common in the natural world as something ordinary and mundane. I needed to rediscover the child's perception within me. Undoubtedly, this is one reason why the Tao Te Ching tells us to "become like a child once more,"[2] and why Jesus is quoted as saying "unless you turn and become like children, you will never enter the kingdom of heaven" (Matt. 18:3).

As a four year old, my daughter did not know the biological mechanisms behind the blooming of a rose. Her intellectual faculties, those associated with logic and sequential thinking, were not yet engaged and, according to psychologists, would not be fully developed until 11 or 12 years of age. She perceived the world mostly through her faculties of intuition, insight and realization. While we often judge them as being unreliable and unscientific, these are the faculties that allow us to experience wonder, to "think outside the box," and break free from the prison of the intellect. For many adults, however, these faculties of insight and realization have gone to sleep. We have been taught to distrust them by our Western academic culture that values science and reason over insight and intuition. Unless we are actively engaged in the arts or have a regular contemplative practice, there is little we are doing to cultivate and appreciate the aesthetic and intuitive dimensions of life.

When Buddhist and Indian philosophers speak of enlightenment as an awakening (the word *Buddha* means "the awakened one"), they are including in that experience, reactivating, through meditation, our mental faculties of insight and realization. During the practice of meditation (see Appendix 1), the silence at the depths of the mind comes to the foreground of our experience while mental activity recedes into the background and can even subside altogether. It is a psycho-physiological experience, simultaneously a condition of heightened awareness and deep relaxation. The Hindu scripture known as the Mandukya Upanishad refers to meditation as the fourth state of consciousness, *Turiya*, which exhibits characteristics distinctly different from our experience of waking, dream and deep sleep.[3]

Think of the mind as being like a pond of water. When left undisturbed, the pond is still and presents us with a clear perception of the images reflecting off its surface. Like the pond, it is the mind's nature to reflect what we take in through the senses, but the tension and fatigue of daily life create "waves" within the mind, causing it to present us with a convoluted image, distorting our perception and our ability to evaluate properly. Meditation is a practice that enables us to restore the mind to its natural condition of tranquility so it can yield a truer reflection of reality.

Besides being a calming experience where we can enjoy a settled mind, meditation involves the experience of deep inner reflection and mindfulness. The mental faculties of reason, logic, and temporal sequential thinking, are momentarily disengaged. We enter what spiritual teachers call the "level of the heart" where our faculties of insight, intuition and realization are "reawakened." Buddhist master Thich Nhat Hanh refers to this as *vipasyana*, meaning "insight" or "looking deeply."[4] Christian contemplative Thomas Merton calls it "interior prayer," which is quite different from verbal prayer. Interior prayer is a process of reflection that involves "not only the mind but also the heart, and indeed our whole being."[5]

During meditation, we witness our thoughts, moods, feelings, and impulses as they arise and subside in the mind on the background of silence. When mental activity subsides during meditation for a significant period, we experience awareness by itself, or "pure consciousness." Through this practice, we develop mindfulness and are awakened to our essential nature, which is beyond the intellect and ego, beyond moods and feelings, indeed, beyond the mind itself.

The experience of mindfulness is of two types, voluntary and involuntary. Voluntary mindfulness occurs by purposeful intention; we purposely direct our awareness to observe a simple task we are performing. Forms of walking meditation often take this approach. Involuntary mindfulness, however, occurs extemporaneously. We become engaged in an activity and unintentionally find ourselves spontaneously witnessing our actions.

Generally, involuntary mindfulness is first experienced during meditation (see Appendix 1) as certain forms of meditation cultivate the witnessing experience, first on the level of thoughts and feelings, and later outside of meditation during waking activity. Eventually, one has the experience of witnessing dreams and deep sleep. The experience of involuntary mindfulness is the long-term result of regular, daily meditation.

In *Walden,* Henry David Thoreau poetically describes this witnessing consciousness which, in the following quote, he refers to as the "spectator."

> However intense my experience, I am conscious of the presence and criticism of a part of me, which as it were, is not a part of me, but spectator, sharing no experience, but taking note of it; and that is no more I than it is you. When the play, it may be the tragedy, of life is over, the

spectator goes his way. It was a kind of fiction, a work of the imagination only so far as he was concerned.[6]

The long-term benefits of meditation, in addition to the physical benefits of deep relaxation and the release of stress, are more profound insights, more frequent realizations, and an improved ability to perceive the interdependence and interconnectedness of all things. We also gain skill in transferring principles from one field of study to another. Realizations lie at the heart of the awakening experience.

In the domain of religion, the experience of awakening is usually associated with Buddhism. The Dhammapada, an important Buddhist scripture, says, "The disciples of Buddha are always well awake."[7] The concept of awakening, however, is also found in Hindu and Christian scripture.

The Katha Upanishad commands the disciple to "arise, awake, sit at the feet of the master and know Brahman."[8] In his letter to the Ephesians, the apostle Paul declares, "Awake, O sleeper and rise from the dead, and Christ will give thee light" (Eph. 5:14). In the Gospel of Mark, Jesus expresses this in the negative, cautioning his disciples not to be caught sleeping: "Watch therefore, for you do not know when the Master of the house will come … lest he come suddenly and find you asleep" (Mark 13:35, 36).

Although I have been quoting mostly from religious texts and the writings of spiritual teachers, the awakening experience is also accessible to the secular humanist. Through the practice of a meditative technique, the awareness is opened to fresh possibilities. Reason is freed from conformity. The mind becomes receptive to the underlying silence deep within, that womb from which insights and realizations are born.

In the apostle Paul's first letter to the Corinthians, we find the metaphor of a trumpet. "Lo! I tell you a mystery. We shall not all sleep, but we shall all be changed, in a moment, in the twinkling of an eye, at the last trumpet. For the trumpet will sound and the dead will be raised imperishable, and we shall be changed" (I Corinthians 15:51, 52).

It has been said that sleep in this passage is a metaphor for death, as if when we die, the soul enters into a deep slumber to be awakened later or in an afterlife. I suggest, however, that there is a deeper meaning intended. Rather than sleep being a metaphor for death, the dead in this passage are a metaphor for those who are unaware and need to be jolted out of their complacency. They are already asleep. There are many people who are biologically alive, but they are aesthetically and spiritually dead. If I walk into a room where you are sleeping and start blowing a trumpet, I guarantee that you will wake up! Paul's trumpet is a metaphor for that which awakens us, and he foresees an age when all of humanity will rise out of the sleep of ignorance to new life.

The Taoist philosopher Chuang Tzu, living in the fourth century BCE, also foresaw such a transformation for humanity when he wrote, "Someday there will be a great awakening when we know that this is all a great dream."[9] Indeed, this has happened on a more limited scale several times already in human history. The Renaissance in Europe, the transition from the geocentric view of the solar system to a heliocentric model, from special creation to evolution, from steady state theory to the Big Bang, from Newtonian physics to general relativity and quantum mechanics, and most recently, the images that have come from the Hubble Space Telescope, and the theory that there may be multiple universes, have brought about periods of awakening that have imposed major paradigm shifts, altering the way we view life and the universe.

In this metaphorical context of awakening, the resurrection of Christ as a literal, historical event becomes a secondary consideration. Given the attention paid to Jesus by religious leaders, politicians, and scholars, Jesus clearly is more alive today than he ever was when he walked the face of the earth. The same can be said for

Buddha, Krishna, and Mohammad, and to a lesser extent for such influential giants as Socrates, Plato, Lao Tsu, Confucius, Aristotle, and many others. They have been granted immortality, and their immortality continues to impact humanity in spite of our willingness or unwillingness to believe.

Science as a Means of Awakening

As the centuries passed, humanity entered what has been called the age of science. This new more systematized approach to gaining knowledge focused on empiricism and the scientific method. Over time, science gained our trust. We had faith that science would solve the mysteries of the universe and decipher all the laws of nature. Using the scientific method, Gregor Johann Mendel (1822–1884), formulated some of the basic principles of heredity. In 1683, Anton van Leeuwenhoek (1632–1723), using the new technology of the microscope, first observed one-celled animals. Some two hundred years later, French chemist Louis Pasteur (1822–1895), would propose that sickness is actually caused by bacteria. His idea challenged the notion that disease is punishment for a person's past sinful deeds.

We are mistaken, however, if we think science relies solely on reason and observation. Our faculties of intuition and insight are as much involved in formulating scientific theory and problem solving as they are in the empirical methods used to test hypotheses.

The Canadian physician and stress researcher Hans Selye*, in addition to his ground-breaking research on biological stress, is

---

* Hans Selye (1907–1982) served on the faculty at McGill University and later at the University of Montreal. He produced well over a thousand also remembered for his book *From Dream to Discovery: On Being a Scientist*. In Chapter 2, he defines intuition as:

> ... the unconscious intelligence that leads to knowledge without reasoning or inferring. It is an immediate apprehension or cognition without rational thought. Intuition is the spark for all forms of originality, inventiveness and ingenuity. It is the flash needed to connect conscious thought with imagination.[10]

Hans Selye (1907-1982)

Selye then includes several examples of how many solutions to problems sought in the laboratory have been triggered by subjective insight. Oftentimes the insights came to the scientist in a dream, or after the researcher had been enjoying a completely unrelated,

---

research papers and was nominated for the Nobel Prize in 1949.

relaxed activity, such as one would have on a fishing trip or while attending a circus.[11] One intriguing example, recounted by Selye, is Otto Loewi's realization of the design of his famous experiment that revealed how nerve impulses are chemically transmitted.

> Otto Loewi ... told me that the idea for his most important experiment came to him one night when he awoke suddenly from sleep. He immediately realized the transcendent importance of the dream and jotted down his thoughts on a piece of paper. But next morning, though aware of having had an inspiration, he could not read his scribble. Try as he would, he was unable to remember what the hunch was until the following night when he again awoke with the same flash of insight as before. This time he tried to arouse himself sufficiently to take legible notes, and the next day he performed his famous experiment on the chemical transmission of nerve impulses.*[12]

After reading this section of Selye's book, it occurred to me that Albert Einstein's ideas about gravity could not have initially come from observation. Einstein explained gravity as the warping of space caused by the mass of an object. Warped space cannot be seen, nor is it an idea that seems "rational." This advance in our understanding of the universe initially came through intuition and insight rather than through the sensory observation. Years later, Einstein's theory would be verified in experiments measuring how a star's light was bent as it passed near the sun during a solar eclipse.

---

* Creative ideas presenting themselves in dreams are reported by musicians and artists as well. When I served on a panel at the International Conference on World Affairs in Boulder, Colorado, songwriter and entertainer Steve Allen told the story of how his most successful song, "This could be the start of something big," came to him in a dream.

With the formulation of quantum mechanics, as well as with theories pertaining to the origin and expansion of the universe, creation is again being seen as filled with mystery. It turns out the axioms we learned in geometry class, and Newton's laws of motion that we used in high school math and science classes, are based on simplistic assumptions. As explained in the previous paragraph, Einstein's revelation that gravitational fields actually warp space-time means it is possible that a line extended far enough in opposite directions, contrary to Euclid's axiom that its ends will never meet, can eventually curve back onto itself and intersect. And with regards to motion, there is always a point of reference somewhere in the universe from which an object that is in motion is perceived to be standing still.

The study of microphysics tells us that matter is comprised mostly of empty space. It is not solid as our senses deceive us into believing. As physicist Leonard Susskind, author of *The Black Hole War*, creatively describes them, the nuclei of atoms "are like soft marshmallows—giant squish balls that are mostly full of empty space."[13]

Experiments in quantum physics demonstrate that a wave on the quantum level behaves like a particle only when an interaction is being observed or recorded. An electron, for example, can be both localized and everywhere at the same time, and behaves differently when it is observed, as if it knows it is being watched. Leonard Susskind explains it as follows: "Until one looks at a particle, or for that matter any other object, there is quantum uncertainty in its location. But once the object is observed, everyone will agree on where it is."[14] When we are not observing, subatomic particles are merely abstract "entities" of energy. That they only behave like particles when their interactions are being measured implies that when we are not observing, the world around us exists in a strange state of interfering wave patterns that is quite indescribable. This is certainly counterintuitive and quite bizarre, but that is the nature of the quantum "field" that underlies our everyday experience which we mistakenly believe to be real.*

This influence of the observer calls into question the assumption at the heart of the scientific method. Why? Because the subject-object duality we experience on this material level of the space-time continuum in which we exist seems like a self-evident truth. On the quantum level, however, this subject-object duality breaks down because the act of observing influences the outcome of the experiment.

What we find is that time is a variable, not a constant; space is curved, not flat. Furthermore, the first law of thermodynamics states that energy is neither created nor destroyed. Energy merely changes form (e.g., from potential energy to kinetic energy). It stands to reason then that the energy which animates our bodies, enlivens the mind, and encodes our individuality, does not simply vanish at the moment of death.

Then there are the phenomena of "entanglement" and "non-locality" at the quantum level. Explained in terms I can understand, it turns out that if two subatomic particles (such as electrons or photons) are allowed to interact, then are separated by a great distance, they remain interconnected such that when one of the particles changes its spin direction (e.g. from up to down), the other particle changes with it (in the example from down to up). This transfer of information between the particles occurs instantaneously, faster than the speed of light. Since nothing travels faster than light, physicists conclude that the particles are interconnected or "entangled." As a wave function, the particles exhibit "non-locality." They are in a sense, interconnected, or one, on the quantum level, as if there were no distance between them. Albert Einstein

---

* For more discussion on the wave to particle collapse in quantum field theory and the role of an "observer," see the section entitled "Singularity as Cosmic Seed" in Chapter 6.

called this phenomenon "spooky." He could not accept the idea of non-locality, nor could he accept the random, probabilistic nature of quantum theory. Despite his skepticism, Einstein's attempts to develop theories that do not rely on this "spooky" behavior were not successful.

Underlying the material realm of existence is a field of infinite potential, and this field is within us as well as all around us. The universe at the quantum level does not behave like it is a predictable mechanistic machine. Rather, it exhibits a random, probabilistic nature, as if it were alive, creative and aware. Astronomer Sir James Hopwood Jeans, who did pioneering work in both astrophysics and quantum mechanics, said it best: "The universe seems to be nearer to a great thought than a great machine."[15]

Let us move now from the very small to the very large.

Since late in the twentieth century, it has been determined that our universe is not only expanding, but its expansion is accelerating. According to astrophysicists, no amount of mass could account for the repulsive force that is causing this acceleration. It is therefore surmised that there must be some unknown form of energy that is causing this exponential expansion. Scientists have appropriately labeled this as *dark energy* since it cannot be seen or detected directly. Leonard Susskind explains that some of our expanding universe may already be beyond our reach.

> In any direction that we look, galaxies are passing the point at which they are moving away from us faster than light can travel. Each of us is surrounded by a cosmic horizon—a sphere where things are receding with the speed of light—and no signal can reach us from beyond that horizon. When a star passes the point of no return, it is gone forever. Far out, at about fifteen billion light-years, our cosmic horizon is swallowing up galaxies, stars, and

probably even life. It is as if we all live in our own private inside-out black hole. …

Are there really worlds like our own that long ago passed through our horizon and became completely irrelevant to anything we can detect? Even worse, is most of the universe forever beyond our knowledge?[16]

While pondering the above quote, I realized that it is as if the cosmos is saying to us—try as you might, you will never catch me, for I will send forth my galaxies at the speed of light. I will expand myself beyond your gaze, and you will never be able to keep up with me.

Realizing this, along with the vast expanse of the universe, I am left awestruck, and am reminded of the words of Rumi, the Sufi poet, when he said, "The real work of religion is permanent astonishment."[17] It is perhaps a similar experience, arrived at through the discipline of science, which moved astronomer Carl Sagan to write:

Science is not only compatible with spirituality; it is a profound source of spirituality. When we recognize our place in an immensity of light-years and in the passage of ages, when we grasp the intricacy, beauty, and subtlety of life, then that soaring feeling, that sense of elation and humility combined, is surely spiritual. So are our emotions in the presence of great art or music or literature, or acts of exemplary selfless courage such as those of Mohandas Gandhi or Martin Luther King, Jr. The notion that science and spirituality are somehow mutually exclusive does a disservice to both.[18]

Living conceptually within Newton's universe led me to believe we had creation pretty much figured out. It felt secure, knowing that the universe behaved in rational, predictable ways. This sense of security I call *egocentric knowing*. We think we know, and rest momentarily in a false sense of knowing as it fulfills a need within us, much like our subconscious desire to align our lives with the changing of the seasons and other cyclical astronomical events that I mentioned at the beginning of this chapter. But much of what we were taught in secondary school, while practical in everyday life experience, has turned out to be illusory.

Nobel prize winning physicist Niels Bohr, in describing the structure of the atom, said "Everything we call real is made of things that cannot be regarded as real."[19] Just when we thought science was giving us the answers, nature has thrown us a curve and hurled us back into the realm of mystery. And after exploring the complex reality of black holes, Leonard Susskind concludes that, "It should be evident that our naïve ideas about space, time and information, are wholly inadequate to understand most of nature."[20] Even the so-called Big Bang holds a mystery that appears unsolvable, as some astronomers have said that the information revealing the cause of this primordial event was most likely destroyed in the explosion.

So I guess the Roman Catholic priest who officiated at the funeral service I attended was right: life, birth, death and the universe will forever be, to some degree, a mystery. Somehow, living organisms emerged in the universe, and explaining how life arose from dead, lifeless matter is much like trying to explain resurrection. We may think we finally have laid this question to rest, whether through insight or reason, in a secure, neat conceptual framework that we have constructed, only to return days later to find the tomb we have placed them in is empty. But this emptiness is a good thing, as it awakens us to renew our search. And this renewal, which we must encounter in our lives many times over, is the spirituality of spring.

CHAPTER 3

The Mystery of Ascension

Among the multitude of animals which scamper, fly, burrow and swim around us, man [sic] is the only one who is not locked into his environment. His imagination, his reason, his emotional subtlety and toughness, make it possible for him not to accept the environment but to change it. And that series of inventions, by which man from age to age has remade his environment, is a different kind of evolution—not biological, but cultural evolution. I call that brilliant sequence of cultural peaks the ascent of man.

—Jacob Bronowski
The Ascent of Man.

Who shall ascend the hill of the Lord?
Who shall stand in his holy place?
He who has clean hands and a pure heart,
Who does not lift up his soul to what is false,
And does not swear deceitfully …

—Psalm 24: 3–4

Ali Akbar Khan (1922–2009) was one of the greatest modern exponents of Hindustani or north Indian classical music. I was fortunate to have had the opportunity to study with the maestro—

affectionately called Khansahib by his students—for nine months at his college of music in San Rafael, California.

Anyone who has even an elementary appreciation for Hindustani music will attest to its aesthetic power. Its hypnotic drone conveys a sense of the primordial origins of creation. Both the Rig Veda and the biblical book of Genesis depict the source of creation using the metaphor of water to convey an image of an infinite ocean of pure existence—the universe in its unmanifest state. Compare, for example, the following passages describing reality just before the process of creation began:

> That One breathed, windless, by its own impulse. Other than that, there was nothing beyond. Darkness was hidden by darkness in the beginning, with no distinguishing sign, all this was water (Rig Veda, 10.129).[1]

> In the beginning, God created the heavens and the earth. And the earth was without form and void, and darkness was on the face of the earth, and the spirit of God was moving over the face of the waters (Gen. 1: 1–3).

On and within this primeval ocean, the primal energy, *prana* in Sanskrit and *ruach* in Hebrew, both of which are associated with spirit and breath, begins to move by virtue of it own nature to express itself, giving rise to the first vibratory impulse. This first impulse is the primordial vibration aurally represented in East Indian music by the underlying tanpura drone. Because the primordial vibration arises on its own accord, it is known as the "unstruck sound" or *Nada Brahman*—the Ultimate Reality in the form of sound. If you listen carefully, you will hear that the tanpura drone is not a static tone. While it is constant in pitch, it is successively increasing and decreasing in amplitude, the changing amplitude coexisting in union with the non-changing pitch, like the waves that rise and fall on an ocean's surface. The aesthetic effect of the tanpura drone captures a sense of this boundless cosmic ocean, leaving one feeling immersed in timelessness, engulfed by the infinite.

From within this undulating drone, the Hindustani soloist manifests a musical creation that begins as an introspective melodic contemplation known as the *alap*. Yet soon it evolves rhythmic life in a section called the *jhor*. This forceful rhythmic movement eventually takes on a cyclical form in a fixed composition called the *gat*. The gat is based on a rhythmic cycle of a specified number of beats, which brings to mind the cyclical experience of the natural world, so important to people living in a pre-industrialized, agrarian society. Hindustani music also follows the cycles of the day and night and of the seasons. Many of its compositions are meant to be performed during a specified season or time of day.

Ali Akbar Khan (1922–2009)

When experiencing India, one cannot help but wonder how such
an elevated and sophisticated art form can co-exist with extreme
poverty and social disarray. It is this paradoxical social condition
that led me to write the following poem during my first trip to India.

> I step between the mirrors of paradox
> In this land that sweats with meaning and gold traditions,
> Where women dress in celebration of silk and color
> And men urinate by the street,
> Where priests burn the sacred camphor to gods as old as light
> And street fires mark the temples of the homeless.
>
> A rickshaw takes me to an evening concert.
> My lungs quarrel with the fumes and dust-filled air.
> A leper petitions me with contorted hands.
> I step into his eyes, even as I depart from his gaze.
>
> At the concert, a sitarist's raga lifts me to a
>   realm where thought disappears,
> Where timeless harmony awakens the primeval song.
> History slips beneath the plane of knowing.
> Antiquity and today are fused into oneness.
>
> The applause jolts me back to a dissonant reality.
> I see myself again, as I try to preserve
>   the silence of centuries.*

Ali Akbar Khan's instrument was the sarode, sometimes referred
to as the Indian lute. He could endlessly manifest melodies with

---

* This poem originally was published in the author's chapbook *In the
Shadow of the Sun: A portrait of India*, published by Jomar Press, 1994.

such depth and infinite variety that one could only marvel at his limitless creativity and sensitive artistry.

One of his long-term American disciples, George Ruckert, who teaches world music classes at the Massachusetts Institute of Technology, told me the story of someone who asked Khansahib if he believed in God. His answer? "I believe in ascending and descending." In an esoteric and amusing way, Ali Akbar Khan was referring to the practice in Indian classical music of ascending and descending the notes of an Indian raga.

Ragas are melodic formulas used to construct melodies for all sorts of genres. They are characterized by mood, an identifying motif or *pakar* that is central to the raga's realization, and a series of five to seven main pitches called *swaras*. There often are complex rules to be observed in the realization of a raga, among them is the proper way to ascend and descend the swaras or main notes. Many ragas require the musician to ascend the raga leaving out certain swaras while including the omitted notes when descending. And sometimes certain notes may be raised during the ascent and lowered when descending, and visa-versa.

On a deeper level of meaning, the proper method of ascending and descending during the exposition of a raga is a metaphor for how we ascend and descend in life. Like waves that rise and subside on the surface of the ocean, people rise and fall during life's journey according to their hard work and virtue, or lack thereof. A person may say that they don't believe in ascension, or the concept of the "fall" as depicted in the myth of Adam and Eve. But we frequently use such imagery in our common everyday language. Historians speak of the rise and fall of empires. Media outlets have written about the "fall" of politicians like Richard Nixon and John Edwards, or how Barrack Obama "ascended" to the U.S. Presidency.

We are not speaking here of a literal physical fall or ascent. Instead, language is being used metaphorically. It is language that comes from the allegorical truth expressed in the myth of Adam's fall

and the redeeming ascension of Christ who the apostle Paul refers
to as the "Last," or Second Adam (1 Cor. 15:45). We fall because
we betray our friends and colleagues, or in the case of politicians,
clergy and other influential people, by transgressing and violating
the trust bestowed upon them by their followers. Conversely, we
"ascend" in life by cultivating within ourselves integrity, compas-
sion, a consistent work ethic and respect for others. As Psalm 26,
quoted at the beginning of this chapter, poetically states, the person
who ascends "the hill of the Lord" must have "clean hands and a
pure heart [and] not lift up his soul to what is false," and "not swear
deceitfully" (Psalm 24: 3–4).

On a psychological and far more personal level however, ascension comes from surrendering, admitting our faults, and removing
the mask we wear when we display our social and professional roles
that so often cover our inadequacies. This includes the process
of relinquishing attachment to outcomes and to our egocentric
desires. Often we experience this after a life crisis has brought us
to a state of feeling abandoned. One enters a metaphorical dark
night where we cannot help but feel forsaken. Surrendering is an
act of humility that brings us down from our inflated false self. If
for no other reason than the realization that there is no other way
to turn, we enter the condition where we let go of our individual
will and our need to control.

From this state of deep repentance one rediscovers the inner voice
which lifts a person to a renewed spiritual awareness. It is the voice
that slays our self-constructed superficial identity, the attachment
to which is what separates us from the Divine Presence. We then
can perceive from a fresh, more holistic and selfless viewpoint, as
if to be lifted up to a new height, not by our own will, but by the
grace of that Divine Power we have surrendered to. One "falls" in
order to be "raised up." Recovering the forgiving embrace of the
Divine Presence is how I describe the experience Fr. Richard Rohr
paradoxically refers to as "falling upward."[2]

People generally harbor two misconceptions about myth. First, they often believe that a myth is something that is false. On the contrary, myth contains truth, but the truth it is expressing is not empirical or historical. Its truth is allegorical and expresses deep emotions fundamental to the human condition and the human psyche. Second, a myth is not something that was supposed to have occurred long ago. Rather, myth is happening all the time. It is an eternal ever-present reality, unfolding each day in our lives.

A view of Lake Michigan and South Manitou Island
off of the coast of Sleeping Bear Dunes

The myth associated with Sleeping Bear Dunes in Michigan is but one example. Many times I have savored the view off the summit of the largest dune, which offers a magnificent panorama of Lake Michigan and two offshore islands accessible only by boat. This beautiful national lakeshore is one of America's natural treasures and, on a vibrant and clear day, delights the mind with its vivid colors.

The dunes are named for a Native American legend of a mother bear and her two cubs that were swimming across Lake Michigan to escape a forest fire. Soon the two cubs grew weary and fell behind. When the mother bear came to the shores of Michigan, she climbed to the highest point she could find, which was a large sand dune, and waited for the cubs. She waited and watched and waited. But her cubs could not make the long journey. Instead, the Great Spirit, who watches over all the animals, turned the cubs into two bodies of land, which are now the North Manitou and South Manitou Islands.

We have in this legend the teaching of life being transformed, but on a more personal level, it expresses what every mother and father must feel who has a lost or missing child. No matter how much closure has been brought to the tragedy, there is always a part of the parent who, like the sleeping bear, is still waiting, clinging to some driftwood of hope that the child might one day return.

Returning now to the myth of Adam's fall, everyday there is someone who falls from an important position of influence because of dishonesty or betrayal; everyday someone somewhere ascends to become an inspiration to others because of discipline, the exercise of virtue and hard work. Explaining and preserving the allegorical meaning of ancient myths is the role of the sage.

Stories of Ascension

There are stories of ascension in the Jewish, Christian and Islamic religious traditions, but interpreting them allegorically rather than as literal, physical events gives them meaning of greater significance. Take, for example, the ascension of Elijah as portrayed in the book of II Kings.

When they had crossed [the river Jordan], Elijah said to Elisha, "Ask what I shall do for you." And Elisha said, "I pray you, let me inherit a double portion of your spirit" … And as they still went on and talked, behold, a chariot of fire and horses of fire separated the two of them. And Elijah went up by a whirlwind into heaven. … Then he [Elisha] took hold of his own clothes and rent them into pieces. And he took up the mantle of Elijah that had fallen from him, and went back and stood on the bank of the Jordan. Then he took the mantle of Elijah that had fallen from him, and struck the water … [and] the water parted to the one side and to the other; and Elisha went over." (II Kings, 2: 9–14).

An understanding of the symbolism in Elijah's ascension in a whirlwind, accompanied by a chariot and horses of fire, reveals that it is not a bodily ascension that is intended. Nor should we conclude that Elijah was scooted off in a space ship flown by ancient astronauts as proposed by UFO enthusiasts. Both wind and fire are ancient symbols for spirit, and the mantle, which Elijah leaves behind, is a metaphor for his prophetic authority, but also his body. His disciple Elisha could then symbolically cross over the water to a new life to carry on and teach in the spirit of Elijah, his spiritual master. Even to this day, when Jews commemorate the Passover, they place an empty chair at the table and open a window or door during their observance so that Elijah's spirit may enter and join them for the Passover meal.

Artists have portrayed the ascension of Christ as Jesus being lifted off the earth into the clouds. This visual glorification, however, is not described as such in the four gospels.* The only mention of

---

* Outside the canonized gospels, there is one descriptive account of the ascension of Christ in the New Testament. This is found in the first chapter of Acts, which is a book written by the same person who wrote

ascension is in the Gospel of John where Jesus tells Mary Magdalene "Do not hold me, for I have not yet ascended to my father" (John 20:17). This is a teaching of nonattachment, a letting go of the master so we can follow our own spiritual path and proceed on that path with confidence. A person must eventually come to know the master on a level far deeper than the master's physical presence in the limited confines of history.

Unfortunately, many interpreters today make the mistake of examining the gospels as if they meant to be a recorded history. In our age of science, this leads to people dismissing such passages as fantasy and thereby missing the allegorical lesson that is intended. Astronomer Carl Sagan once anecdotally told Episcopal Bishop John Shelby Spong that if Jesus ascended into heaven 2000 years ago travelling at the speed of light, he'd still be in our galaxy![3]

Theologians, clergy and scientists considering the ascension of Jesus as literal are as misguided as philosophers would be if they

---

the Gospel of Luke and considered by some theologians to be a sequel to Luke's gospel (see Acts 1: 9–11).

One would think Jesus being lifted off the earth into the sky would be an incredibly dramatic and stunning event to those disciples who witnessed it. But this miraculous "exit" is recorded in a way that seems rather routine. In merely one short sentence, Jesus is described as simply being "lifted up," then removed from their sight by a cloud. Afterwards, two men in white robes stood beside them, saying that Jesus would return in the same way that he departed.

An allegorical interpretation of these verses suggests that Jesus was to be symbolically "lifted up" before the world. But how his life would become elevated and made significant in the context of history was, to his disciples, an unknown. After his humiliating and tortuous crucifixion, any vision of his life becoming influential to the point that it would mark the beginning of a new era on the world calendar was surely well beyond their sight, as if metaphorically hidden by a cloud.

examined Plato's "Allegory of a Cave" as if it were an actual event in history. Imagine scholars asking where the cave was in Greece, or how many prisoners there might have been, or whether the Greeks actually chained their prisoners in caves so they could only see their shadows. Such explorations, or rejections, of stories meant to be understood as allegories, are not at all what their authors intended.

We can further see that Jesus was not speaking of literal ascension by examining the way he viewed heaven. In the book of Revelation, the author describes the heavenly "New Jerusalem" as descending from the heavens onto the earth (Rev. 21:2). It is clearly evident in the gospels, however, that Jesus sees heaven, *not* as a celestial city, but as a new way of perceiving the world. He does not see it as a literal place outside us, or as an experience enjoyed only by departed souls. Consider, for example, the following passages:

> The kingdom of heaven is not coming in signs to be observed; nor will they say "Lo, here it is!" or "There!" for behold, the Kingdom of God is in your midst [or within you] (Luke 17:21).*

> The Kingdom of Heaven is like a treasure hidden in a field, which a man found and covered up, then in his joy goes and sells everything he owns and buys that field (Matt. 13:34).

---

* The Revised Standard Version of the Bible translates the last phrase of this passage as "the kingdom of God is in your midst." The original Greek text, as found in the Alfred Marshall Interlinear Greek-English New Testament, reads "within you," rather than "in your midst." Despite the difference in translations, either rendering depicts heaven as an immediate and accessible reality rather than as a place enjoyed only by departed souls.

> Whoever does not receive the kingdom of God like a child shall not enter it (Mark 10:15).

> When you make the two into one, and when you make the inner like the outer and the outer like the inner, and the upper like the lower, and when you make male and female like a single one, so that the male will not be male nor the female be female ... then you will enter the Kingdom [of Heaven] (The Gospel of Thomas, verse 22).

The last quote above is from the Gospel of Thomas which, along with numerous Gnostic texts, is one of the manuscripts discovered in Egypt near Nag Hammadi in 1948. The contemporary group of scholars known as *The Jesus Seminar* includes the Gospel of Thomas in their book entitled *The Five Gospels*. In this verse from the Gospel of Thomas, Jesus is clearly referring to a change in our perception of reality that is more akin to what in philosophy is called a "paradigm shift." Our world is as if "turned upside down" or, "inside out." During a paradigm shift, the view of life we have constructed, whether it be a perspective that is localized to the domain of our individual life circumstances, or one that is broad enough to be defined as a worldview, is suddenly drastically altered. We are then confronted with a cognitive dissonance that forces us to redefine ourselves and our place in the universe.

On the broadest level, changes in our paradigm can result from a new and revolutionary scientific theory or discovery. The shift from the geocentric view of the solar system to the heliocentric model, from special creation to evolution, from steady state theory to the expanding universe, and from Newtonian physics to general relativity and quantum mechanics, are but a few examples. All of these new paradigms have one thing in common: the reality they present is increasingly counterintuitive to our everyday experience.

On a personal level, a paradigm shift can be triggered by the death of an influential person in our life, such as is being depicted in the book of II Kings where Elisha experiences the passing of Elijah. To be granted a portion of the master's spirit, he must let go of the master, and realize that his master's presence and influence upon him is independent of his physical form. Jesus is teaching Mary Magdalene to let go when he says, "Do not hold me" (John 20:17). And the apostles receive a portion of their master's spirit when the Holy Spirit, again depicted symbolically through the image of fire accompanied by the sound of rushing wind (Acts 2:1–4), descends upon the apostles on the day of Pentecost. The manifest, physical form of the master is but a limited, finite expression of the transcendent wisdom that he or she embodied.

Ascension Brought Down to Earth

Cultural anthropologist Jacob Bronowski, in his book and public television series, *The Ascent of Man*, documents the rise of human civilization through technological and scientific achievements. To accomplish this technological progress, the human species had to develop the ability to forgo the gratification of a desire. To construct a weapon to slay a deer, we must delay the fulfillment of the desire to eat the deer long enough to construct the weapon. Thus, advancement in cultural evolution is dependent on discipline and the ability to delay gratification. Each era of advancement is like scaffolding on which a new level of achievement can be built.[4]

The twentieth century, however, saw two ruthless world wars that set humanity's economic and cultural progress back by decades. The question must be asked: will humanity continue to ascend to new heights in the twenty-first century as the high-tech revolution continues to advance? Or will we descend into economic and cultural ruin once again?

If humanity is to further its ascent, we must not allow war to continue to be our legacy. We must learn to resolve conflicts applying the principles of nonviolent resistance as taught by Mahatma Gandhi and Rev. Dr. Martin Luther King, Jr. We must master the art of fighting injustice using nonviolent strategies, and structure economic and political systems that build a positive, transformative peace between nations. It remains to be seen, however, whether humanity can ascend to its rightful place in the universe and be an example to other civilizations we may one day discover in our galaxy.

I would like to conclude this chapter with two down-to-earth examples of ascension, the first being that of Oprah Gail Winfrey, who told her remarkable story in an hour-long interview with David Letterman at Ball State University on November 26, 2012.[5]

Growing up in rural Mississippi in the late 1950s and 60s, Oprah recounted how she was abused as a child—beaten with a switch until welts appeared on her thighs and blood ran down her leg, yet told to not show her feelings; sexually molested and raped by age nine. At age 14 she became pregnant and gave birth to a boy who died soon after he was born.

When she lived in Milwaukee, Wisconsin, her mother, in trying to cope with Oprah's unruly behavior, took her to a detention home for "bad girls." While sitting, waiting to be admitted, she was devastated at the possibility of having to live at this home. She thought to herself, "God, how did this happen to me. Please help me." Soon thereafter the supervisor came into the office to tell her that she could not stay because they had no room.

Oprah describes this as a defining "life-saving moment". She then moved to Tennessee where she attended high school. She made a choice to change her life's direction, and by age 16, was elected president of the student council, competed on the debate team, and excelled in public speaking which enabled her to win a scholarship to Tennessee State University. She also gained experience in radio broadcasting. This launched her media career that ultimately blossomed into her immensely popular television show that originated in Chicago. She became the first African-American woman to host a nationally televised talk show.

Oprah Winfrey ascended from a life of poverty and abuse to become one of the wealthiest and most influential women in history. Her generous philanthropic efforts have extended her influence throughout the world. Perhaps the most notable is her creation of the Oprah Winfrey Leadership Academy for Girls in South Africa which was opened in January of 2007.

In her interview with David Letterman on the Ball State University campus, Oprah spoke of being "spiritually fed" through her church experience as a young child. That exposure, along with her discipline and determined will, helped her overcome adversity to succeed in a society where in her childhood, life's many currents were going against her.

The second example of down-to-earth ascension is that of legendary baseball player Leroy "Satchel" Paige, who Joe DiMaggio described as "the best fastball pitcher I ever faced." Paige was the third African-American to play in the major leagues, following Jackie Robinson and Larry Doby.

The movie "Don't Look Back," which tells the story of his life, begins with Paige, who was born into a poor family in Alabama, carrying suitcases at a train station. It is from this humble boyhood occupation that he earned both tips and his nickname. His last name was originally spelled P-a-g-e, but his mother changed it to P-a-i-g-e as she believed it would give the family name more class.

After a few encounters with the law, which included petty theft and truancy, Satchel was arrested for shoplifting and sent to a reform school for black youths where he spent five years. It is there that he played baseball and learned to pitch. After his release from reform school, Paige tried out for the Negro Leagues. This was the "separate but equal" era in the United States. He spent most of his baseball career playing in the Negro Leagues where he built his reputation as a fastball pitcher.

Satchel's reputation became a permanent fixture in baseball history in one particular game when, in the ninth inning, the bases became loaded with two outs due to three consecutive outfielder errors. Satchel became so disgusted he called in his outfielders and told them all to sit down. Then, despite jeers and boos from the crowd, he proceeded to strike out the last batter, winning the game.

In 1947, Bill Veeck, owner of the Cleveland Indians, gave Satchel his chance in the Major Leagues amidst much controversy. There had never been a black pitcher in the Major Leagues. When considering whether or not to have Paige try out for the team, legend has it that Veeck placed his cigarette butt on the ground to serve as home plate. He then asked Paige to throw 6 pitches at this minuscule target. Five of the pitches were perfect strikes!

That year Paige was instrumental in helping Cleveland win the American League pennant race. The movie on his life ends with Paige walking out to the mound as a relief pitcher in the World Series in front of thousands of fans.

Satchel Paige: from poverty, to reform school, to the segregated Negro leagues, to helping break the color barrier in the Majors, and ultimately, to pitching in the 1948 World Series. That, my friends, is ascension.

Satchel Paige (1906–1982)

Chapter 4

From Soma Sacrifice to Eucharist

I am the origin of the whole world and also its dissolution. …
I am the beginning, the middle, and also the end of all beings.
—Krishna
Bhagavad Gita, 7:6; 10:20)

I am the Alpha and the Omega, the first and the last, the
beginning and the end.

—Jesus
Rev. 22:13

Behold the whole world of moving and unmoving things,
united in my body.

—Krishna
Bhagavad Gita, 11:7.

For he has made known to us in all wisdom and insight the
mystery of his will … to unite all things in him [Christ],
things in heaven and things on earth.

—The apostle Paul
Ephesians 1:9–10

Each morning in New Delhi I would wake up to an alluring saffron-colored sky. The cloud of pollution does seem to have its silver lining. Every two or three days after finishing my breakfast, I would walk about a mile through a myriad of colors, sounds and smells, to the residence of Diam Ali Qadri. I was in New Delhi to study tabla thanks to a generous grant from the Eli Lilly Endowment, and Diam Ali Qadri had gained an international reputation as a master of the tabla.

The tabla is the most sophisticated hand-drumming instrument in the world. Anyone who hears a performance of Hindustani music can't help but be amazed at the skill and virtuosity displayed by a tabla master. Without a doubt, my teacher was very deserving of that title, especially since he had performed with sitarist Ravi Shankar and other well-known Hindustani musicians.

Maestro Qadri lived in a humble dwelling near Connaught Place. Each morning when I arrived at his house, I would be greeted by his 16 year-old son who was already quite accomplished at playing his father's instrument.

One morning, while his son was putting me through my musical paces in preparation for his father to enter and begin my lesson, I was told I could not have my lesson in two days because of a wedding his family had to attend. I could tell from the tone of his voice that his son was not excited about going.

"It's my cousin who is getting married. It will be a long event—a Muslim wedding that will last all day. I wish it were a Christian wedding. I think they are shorter. Besides," he continued, "I don't like the guy she's marrying."

I was stunned at how familiar his words sounded. Complaints about in-laws, or in this case, a future in-law, and about lavish weddings made me suddenly realize how such feelings are not unique to my own family and culture. While culture is important, and appreciating traditions outside our comfort zone is vital to cross-cultural understanding, it is also somewhat superficial. There is a deeper level of humanity, of personal needs and feelings, that inevitably breaks through the façade of culture once you get to know someone in a deeper, more personal way.

In response, I first corrected his generalization that all Christian weddings were shorter as I briefly described my high school friend's Polish-Italian wedding that I ushered for many years ago. It was an occasion that lasted from ten o'clock in the morning to midnight!

The words of my tabla teacher's son were just the beginning of a penetrating thought process that eventually led me to uncover common themes and symbols hidden within the teachings found in Hindu, Buddhist, Jewish and Christian cultures. The old adage "East is East and West is West" is an assumption on which much of Western philosophical and religious thought has been based. This assumption is false, and I soon found ample evidence to demonstrate how mistaken we have been to accept it. Included in this evidence are highly similar verses, symbols, metaphors and teachings found in Hindu and Christian scriptures (in addition to those quoted at the beginning of this chapter). Furthermore, there is meaning behind the symbolism that is revealed when comparing the Christian Eucharist with a ritual known as the soma sacrifice described in the Hindu scripture, the Rig Veda. It is not so much that the twains will eventually meet, but that, in actuality, they were never separated.

The sacrament of the Lord's Supper, referred to in orthodox Christian circles as the Holy Eucharist, is central to worship in many Christian denominations. More commonly known as communion, it consists of believers in attendance partaking of the body and blood of Christ as present in the elements of bread and wine (many protestant denominations substitute grape juice for wine). This ritual has become so identified with Christian worship that it may seem to many to be a Christian innovation. Theologians point out, however, that the ritual has historical roots that predate the Christian era by hundreds of years. According to A. Powell Davies, pre-Christian rituals for connecting with the spiritual presence of a deity involved the use of fermented drinks made from grains such as wheat and barley.

> It had been noticed that water in which cereals had been placed would sometimes acquire strange qualities. This was the work of the god. The chemistry of the fermentation was of course not understood and the change that had taken place in the liquid was therefore unaccountable on any natural basis. When the liquid was imbibed it was self-evident that the power of the god was in it because of the effect it had on those who drank it. Hence the worshipers were said to be *enthused* the literal meaning of which is *filled with the god.*[1]

That bread was baked from these same grains makes it easy to see how bread would become associated with the body of the god. Similarly, when grapes were used to make the fermented drink, the juice or "blood" of the grape came to represent the life-force of the deity.[2]

The association of life-force with blood was also found in Mithraism, a mystery religion based on the mythological slaying of a bull, and its ritual included a ritual using bread and wine. Mithraism was Christianity's chief rival up to about the fourth century, and its history extends back "many centuries before the Christian era into India and Persia."[3] Even today, one can find a statue of a bull in temples throughout India, particularly those dedicated to Shiva. This connection of Mithraism with India, and the fact that it rivaled the early Church and predated Christianity by several centuries, suggests that the sacrament involving bread and fermented drink may have an even more ancient origin.

The Soma Sacrifice

The Vedic soma sacrifice is one of the great mysteries in ancient sacred literature. Numerous hymns (poems) are devoted to soma in the Rig Veda, a text sacred to Hindus believed to have its origins in Indo-European oral tradition dating back 4000 years. In the ceremonial rite described in the Rig Veda, the soma plant, said to grow near the mountain tops, is gathered and sacrificed, with "pressing stones" being used to squeeze the golden juice out of its stalk. The juice is then filtered through a fleece, mixed with water, and drunk to achieve a state of transcendent unity with a deity.[4]*

Today, the soma sacrifice is no longer practiced in Hinduism, and the knowledge and specific whereabouts of the renowned soma plant has been lost. According to Hindu legend, the powerful, inspirational and prophetic influence of soma prompted the creator deity *Brahma* to banish soma to the outer regions of the universe where only the gods have access to it. As a result, humans could only acquire soma through the sunbird or phoenix, the mythological bird which flies to earth from heaven, dies, resurrects from its ashes, then ascends back to heaven, leaving the soma behind. Thus, in orthodox Hinduism, the soma sacrifice is believed to have been lost and is, therefore, no longer practiced. The concept of soma and its corresponding ritual, however, have been kept alive in two other religious traditions: Zoroastrians who include in their devotions the "drink of immortality," and Christians who observe the rite of communion.

While in many Vedic hymns soma is referred to as a sacred plant, several other images are associated with soma, images that also are

---

*   It may also be that the "golden fleece," which Jason and the Argonauts search for in the well-known Greek legend, is meant to be the sieve used in the ancient Vedic ritual.

found in Jewish scripture, particularly in the book of Exodus. The Rig Veda likens soma to the "pillar of the sky;"[5] Exodus 13:21–22 refers to the pillar of smoke and fire in the sky that led the Israelites out of Egypt. Soma is equated with milk and honey,[6] symbols in the Rig Veda for fertility and wealth; the book of Exodus, verses 3:8; 13:5; and 33:3, describes the Promised Land as a "land flowing with milk and honey" (see Chapter 2 for an explanation of this symbolism).

The Vedic hymns also associate soma with the eagle;[7] the same image is again found in Exodus 19:4 where God reminds the Israelites how, "I bore you on eagles' wings and brought you to myself." The phoenix or sunbird as it is referred to in the Rig Veda, is symbolized by the eagle, which is said to bring soma to earth from the heavens on its wings as the fiery juice of immortality.[8] The phoenix image is also used to describe the messiah in the Hebrew book of Malachi, "the Sun of Righteousness shall rise with healing in its wings" (Malachi 4: 1, 2).* Soma is further associated with a "whirlwind" and with the sage who heals,[9] images used also to describe the Hebrew prophet Elijah who healed the sick and was caught up in a whirlwind and taken up into heaven in a chariot of fire (II Kings 2:11)†. In addition, soma is said to be that inner source of poetry and scripture which inspires the seers (prophets).[10]

Some researchers have become convinced that soma was an actual biological plant. A more thorough reading of the soma hymns in the Rig Veda, and the many images surrounding the concept, suggest that soma was not a literal substance but a metaphor for experiences associated with the internalization of mystical teachings resulting from spiritual enlightenment. In this case the sacred drink represents that teaching which has become part of one's being, absorbed,

---

*   In this passage from Malachi, "wings" is sometimes translated as "rays," as if the rays of the rising sun are its wings.

†   See Chapter 3, section entitled "Stories of Ascension".

like food, into a person so one can spontaneously live and express the teaching in daily life. The Law becomes written on one's heart, as it says in the book of the prophet Jeremiah.*

Soma may also have been the ancient way of poetically describing the elevated experience of bliss or wholeness during the contemplative state of samadhi or transcendental consciousness, an experience which today is known to be accompanied by bio-chemical changes in the physical body. In a poem I wrote years ago, I attempted to capture this contemplative experience of samadhi where the mind is fully absorbed in the soma-light that ascends within the body to flood the mind, leaving one in a state of rapture.

> Rhyme sweeps away time.
> scattering darkness as the
> poet blesses language with
> the sacred breath.
>
> The fountain of soma light
> ascends to flood the mind,
> a naked brightness untamed.
>
> Leave behind sight and sound.
> Wrap your words in sandalwood
> carved into the silence where
> wisdom speaks unchallenged,
> stirring the slumber of sages.

---

* "I will put my law within them, and I will write it upon their hearts ..." (Jer. 31:33). The spontaneous beating of the heart is governed by the involuntary nervous system and is not under the direct control of our individual will. It is an appropriate symbol for a teaching that has been absorbed so completely that it is naturally expressed in one's life, much like what occurs when a person has learned to speak a language fluently.

As introduced in Chapter 2, another association made in the Rig Veda is soma's connection with fertility and wealth as symbolized by milk and honey. In this poetic context, milk is not cow's milk but rather, the rain that is "milked" from the clouds.[11] The association with honey is made because of its sweet taste, but also due to its golden color and the color of the stalks from which the juice is extracted. These associations with fertility and wealth suggest a more practical, agrarian meaning should be ascribed to the biblical phrase "a land flowing with milk (rain) and honey (wealth)" (Exodus 3:8), the words used to describe the land God promised to the Israelites.

In addition to these associations with fertility and wealth, soma is also depicted in the Rig Veda as a "sage" who heals the sick and as a king who makes intercession with the gods.

1. This restless Soma—you try to grab him but he breaks away and overpowers everything. He is a sage and a seer inspired by poetry.
2. He covers the naked and heals all who are sick. The blind man sees; the lame man steps forth.
3. Soma, you are the broad defense against those who hate us, both enemies we have made ourselves and those made by others …
4. Be kind and merciful to us, Soma; be good to our heart, without confusing our powers in your whirlwind.
5. King Soma, do not enrage us; do not terrify us; do not wound our heart with dazzling light.
6. Give help, when you see the evil plans of gods in your own house. Generous king, keep away hatreds, keep away failures (Rig Veda, 8th Mandala, Hymn 79).[12]

The soma sacrifice is thus transformed into the sacrifice of the sage, and from the Christian perspective, the sage that is sacrificed is Jesus Christ. And it is Christ who, for the Christian, intercedes with God the Father to give strength in the face of evil and temptation.

Theologians have recognized that the writers of the New Testament often combined images and bridged languages using the device of a play on words. John Allegro, author of *The Dead Sea Scrolls and the Christian Myth*, explains how the imagery of Christ as the "Lamb of God" in the Gospel of John and the book of Revelation is "an ingenious piece of word-play", relating Aramaic *imera*, meaning "lamb," with Hebrew *imerah*, meaning "word." This literary device combines Christ's sacrificial earthly role as the Passover lamb with his pre-existent metaphysical status as the Logos or Word, the cosmic Creative Principle.[13]*

In a similar way, an inter-linguistic play-on-words is also present in the word soma. The term soma, while referring to an intoxicating drink in Sanskrit, means "body" in Greek. In the letters of the apostle Paul, the term is applied when speaking of the metaphysical "spiritual" body as well as the mortal, perishable physical one.

----

* The Greek *logos*, from which comes the English term "logic," carries the dual meaning of reason and speech. It implies a dialectic process of teaching and learning which leads the student to understanding a philosophical or spiritual truth through reasoned dialog. In the opening verse of the Gospel of John, however, Logos is given a divine status: "In the beginning was the Word (Logos), and the Word was with God and the Word was God" (John, 1:1). This is an extension of the idea found in Jewish scripture where it is through the Creator's speech that creation is brought forth: "And God *said*, 'Let there be light,' and there was light" (Gen. 1:3—italics mine), and "By the word of the Lord the heavens were made, and all their host by the breath of his mouth ... . For He spoke and it came to be, he commanded and it stood forth" (Psalm 33:6–9). As a further extension, Logos in Christian theology became associated with Divine Reason, which is made known through the Word (i.e. speech) of the Christ who is the embodiment of that Word which has the power to manifest a new creation, the new creation being a new paradigm or way of redefining and conceptually reorganizing the world as we experience it.

"So it is with the resurrection of the dead. What is sown
is perishable; what is raised is imperishable." It is sown
in dishonor; it is raised in glory ... It is sown in physical
body; it is raised in a spiritual body ..." (I Cor. 15:42–44).

In modern-day popular Christianity, however, the common usage
of the term "body," as in the phrase "Body of Christ," is generally
limited to the physical collection of believers that comprise the
Church. It is a context analogous to such familiar phrases as "legisla-
tive body" or "congressional body." This generally is the interpretation rendered for a passage such as Romans 12:4–5.

"For as in one body we have many members, and all the
members do not have the same function, so we, though
many, are one body in Christ, and individually members
one of another."

Nevertheless, there is the metaphysical dimension to the concept
of body, and in particular the "Body of Christ" that is equally
applicable to the preceding passage but mostly overlooked. This
metaphysical dimension is the body (soma) that Christians, by one
Spirit, are said to be baptized into, and are "made to *drink* of the
spirit" (I Cor. 12:13; italics are mine).

"[Christ] is the image of the invisible God, the first-born of
all creation, for in whom all things were created, in heaven
and on earth, visible and invisible ... all things were created
through him and for him." (Col. 1:15; also see John 1:1–3)

This is the Christ that existed in the beginning with God, poetically expressed as the "first born of all creation," through whom
all things came into being, and to whom, according to Christian
theology, the cosmos has been given over to in love.

The Metaphysical Body

To understand the metaphysical dimensions of the Body of Christ, we must look into pre-Christian history to the theologies of Gnosticism and the Essenes. The Gnostics and the Essenes were mystery religions or cults that existed within the Greek and Jewish traditions respectively. They are called "mystery religions" because they taught that divine truth was personally accessible to each individual. One prepared for this vision of the "Knowledge of God" through esoteric practices designed to reveal the kingdom of God to the devotee through direct revelation.[14] It was a concept that is not unlike the "secrets of the kingdom of heaven" spoken of in Matthew 13:11, or what the apostle Paul refers to when he writes, "we impart a secret and hidden wisdom of God, which God decreed before the ages for our glorification" (I Cor. 2:7), or which Paul calls the "mystery of Christ," made known by revelation (Ephesians 3:3–4).

Both the Gnostics and the Essenes taught a variant of the "Myth of the Primordial Adam," that there existed in the beginning of creation a primordial spiritual body of light in the form of a heavenly primeval man. Creation began with the breaking up of this primeval body by the forces of darkness into pieces of light, each piece becoming the innermost self of anyone born into the physical world.[15] In time, a redeemer was to appear who would gather all the pieces of light together again, restoring the primeval spiritual body.

There are many examples of this imagery found in the Jewish and Christian Testaments. God's first act of creation is the creation of light (Genesis 1:3). Christ as the "first-born of all creation" (Col. 1:15) is the personification of that primordial light manifesting as the "light of the world." Through him, Christians are said to become "children of the light" (John 12:36; I Thessalonians 5:5; Luke 16:8) and to abide in him as he (the light) abides in them (John

15:4). Furthermore, theologians recognize that Greek Gnosticism influenced a significant amount of the apostle Paul's theology.[16] The primeval man referred to in the Gnostic myth is quite possibly the concept Paul is alluding to when he writes, "we shall also bear the image of the man of heaven" (I Cor. 15:49). In addition, Paul writes in his letter to the Ephesians of God's plan to "unite all things in him [Christ], things in heaven and things on earth" (Ephesians 1:10).

This belief in the restoration of a primeval metaphysical body of souls may express a deep-seated subconscious desire within each of us for reuniting humanity. Throughout history many ethnic groups have experienced a diaspora, a scattering of tribes and relatives which takes its toll on family cohesion and cultural identity. In some instances this was the natural result of people leaving their homeland to pursue educational or economic opportunities elsewhere; in other circumstances it was people fleeing oppression or concealing their ethnic heritage to avoid social prejudice or persecution. This last reason was the case with my father.

Until his death in 1987, my father always said he was of German descent. But in 2013, my brother had his DNA analyzed. The analysis revealed that my father's paternal ancestors were Ashkenazi, which was a European Jewish population that lived in the Alsace region which is now eastern France. In the 1920's, my dad changed the spelling of his name, adding the "E" to W-O-L-F to conceal his Jewish heritage. Wolf without the "e" added is a common Jewish spelling, as is also the spelling W-O-L-F-F. Wolfe with the "e" is characteristically English or Irish. Residing in the United States well before WWI, my father's situation was not one of having to survive Nazi persecution. Yet, certainly part of the reason he concealed his Jewish heritage was to elude the scourge of anti-semitism, as well as hate groups in the United States like the Ku Klux Klan. I suspect he was also trying to protect my brother, born in 1937, should fascism ever reach the shores of America.

In addition to our predominantly Jewish and German ancestry, my brother's DNA analysis also showed we had inherited genetic material from populations in Sub-Saharan Africa, Italy, and the United Kingdom, and that we were 3% Neanderthal. The relevant message from this knowledge of our genetic heritage is that the concept of race in classifying humans is obsolete. DNA analysis demonstrates that we are all related. There are no "pure bloodlines." There is only one race, and that is the human race. We are all cousins, with the same variety of blood types, and the same genetic code.

Several religious traditions have emerged in past centuries as well-meaning efforts to unite diverse traditions and cultural groups as a way of healing the wounds of diaspora. The movement inspired by the nineteenth century sage Ramakrishna in India who taught the unity of all religions, and the Baha'i faith, the motto for which is "Mankind is One," are two examples. I would argue that this was an original intent of Christianity until the religion became politicized in the fourth century when it was made a state religion by the Roman Emperor Constantine.

Take for example the apostle Paul's words in his letter to the church in Galatia that in Christ, "there is neither Jew nor Greek, there is neither slave nor free, there is neither male and female" (Gal. 3:28). It also appears that Jesus, in his telling of the parable of the Good Samaritan (Luke 10:30–35) was trying to heal the schism between the Samaritans, who were people of Jewish descent who had intermarried with other populations, and the Jewish population in Jerusalem. Unfortunately, the need for individual tribal identity and political influence continues to overrule efforts to bring diverse peoples together. We constantly struggle to instill the view that we all are members of one human family, regardless of religion or ethnicity, while at the same time we continually create obstacles to seeing ourselves as a global community. In a familiar gospel parable, Jesus tells of a man who held a huge wedding banquet.

Many people were invited to join together in celebration, but they all declined (Luke 14:15–24; Matt. 22:8–10). Like the invited guests in this parable, we are good at making excuses as to why we cannot attend opportunities to come together and share a meal in the spirit of reconciliation.

The Essene and Gnostic myths of the primordial Adam pre-date Christianity, but the earliest known rendition of the primordial spiritual "man" is the myth of Purusha found in the Rig Veda. In Indian philosophy, Purusha is the cosmic spirit or soul. Hymn 90 of the 10th Mandala of the Rig Veda depicts Purusha as a giant primeval man, the "ruler of immortality," who is bound and sacrificed by the gods to bring forth creation.

1. The Man has a thousand heads, a thousand eyes, a thousand feet. He pervaded the earth on all sides and extended beyond it as far as ten fingers.

2. It is the Man who is all this, whatever has been and whatever is to be. He is the ruler of immortality. …

3. Such is his greatness, and the Man is yet more than this. …

6. When the gods spread the sacrifice with the Man as the offering, spring was clarified butter, summer the fuel, autumn the oblation.

7. They anointed the Man, the sacrifice born at the beginning, upon the sacred grass. …

11. When they divided the Man, into how many parts did they apportion him? ...

13. The moon was born from his mind; from his eye the sun was born. Indra and Agni came from his mouth, and from his vital breath the Wind was born.

14. From his naval the middle realm of space arose; from his head the sky evolved. From his two feet came the earth,

and the quarters of the sky from his ear. Thus they set
the worlds in order.

15. There were seven enclosing-sticks for him, and thrice
seven fuel-sticks, when the gods, spreading the sacrifice,
bound the Man as the sacrificial beast.

16. With the sacrifice the gods sacrificed to the sacrifice.
These were the first ritual laws.[17]

In the above hymn, the image of Purusha, spread out for the
sacrifice and bound like the sacrificial beast, is easily transferred
to Christ being stretched out and bound to the cross. Furthermore,
it states that the "gods sacrificed to the sacrifice." Paradoxically,
Purusha is that which is sacrificed, but he is also the divinity to
which the sacrifice is made; that is, he is both the subject and object
of the sacrifice.[18] The same can be said for the sacrifice of Christ
on the cross. Jesus as the incarnate form of God and as the paschal
"Lamb of God" (John 1:29) is the subject to which the sacrifice,
including his own, is made.

In this sense, the sacrifice of Christ alludes to the descriptive
imagery of the Purusha myth. Christ's metaphysical or spiritual
body, as it existed in the beginning as the "first-born of all creation"
is broken up, the light being scattered like sheep from a shepherd's
fold. At the culmination of his earthly manifestation, he is stretched
out and bound for the sacrifice made in his crucifixion.

Early Christian writers transformed the ancient soma sacrifice
using a clever play on words that bridged the languages of Sanskrit
and Greek. For the word "soma" in Greek means "body." Thus
the "soma sacrifice," while in Vedic Sanskrit refers to the sacrifice
of a plant for its juice, in Christianity becomes the sacrifice of
the Body (soma) of Christ, whose life, death, resurrection and
ascension reflect the life of the mythological phoenix or sunbird,
whose destiny is to bring the soma to earth. Moreover, in the

Christian Eucharist, the sacrifice is celebrated in a way similar to the description of the Vedic rite; i.e., juice is pressed from a plant (grapes), is mixed with water, then drunk to gain mystical union with the Divine, which in Christianity is Christ's spiritual body (soma). The juice, however, is now red rather than golden to represent the blood Christ shed during the sacrifice of his "soma," and the water the priest adds to the wine symbolizes the water (in addition to blood) that flowed from the side of the crucified Christian avatar.

Through the Vedic reference to soma as both the elixir of immortality and the sage, and through the interpolation permitted by the meaning of the word soma in the Greek language, the soma sacrifice now becomes transferred from a polytheistic context in Hinduism, through an idyllic context in pre-Christian Mithraism, to a monotheistic context centered around Jesus Christ who, in Christianity, is God incarnate. By means of this sacrament, the mystical union of the disciples with the avatar, sent as the light in an age of darkness, could be symbolized and subsequently presented in ritual. Given its heritage, the meaning of this ritual within Christianity becomes extremely potent, much more so than most Christians recognize.

Thus the ancient soma sacrifice, which Hindus believe was lost ages ago, was revived and given new meaning by early Christian writers, and ironically (unbeknownst to most modern-day Hindus), is currently being practiced on a weekly basis in churches around the world.

CHAPTER 5

The Mystery of Inner Space

*Every man [sic] is a builder of a temple, called his body, to
the god he worships, after a style purely his own, nor can he
get off by hammering marble instead. We are all sculptures
and painters, and our material is our own flesh and blood
and bones. Any nobleness begins at once to refine a man's
features, any meanness or sensuality to imbrute him.*

—Henry David Thoreau
from *Walden*

We wake, if ever at all, to mystery.

—Annie Dillard

Adams County, Ohio is home to a fascinating earthwork known
as Serpent Mound. Built by Native Americans sometime in the
eleventh century, it stretches a little over a quarter of a mile, winding
its way along a hillside until a person finds its open mouth, which
appears poised to devour what looks like an egg. The meaning
behind this earthwork is still a mystery, but my own conjecture
is that it was built to represent the regenerative force in nature.
The serpent has long been a symbol for the cyclical structure of
creation, an unfolding process undergoing perpetual transformation and continual death and renewal, year after year, generation
after generation.

Since the beginning of civilization, humans have had a need for sacred gathering places—spaces designated for the worship of the forces in the universe that are beyond the human mind's ability to fully grasp. Originally, such gathering places appear to have been unconfined, open and integrated into the natural world. They were often set in relation to the movement of the sun, moon and stars, and left subject to the elements with which the devotee was to seek harmony.

Another noted example is Stonehenge in southern England. Some scholars assert that its design aligns with the movement of the sun and moon along the horizon, providing seasonal knowledge that was important to agrarian and hunter-gatherer tribes.[1] There are many other ancient sacred spaces and altars around the world. Those mentioned in the oldest scriptures, the Rig Veda, the Epic of Gilgamesh, and the five books of Moses, are described as open-air altars.*

In my study of religious traditions, I have noticed that as cultures developed masonry skills, sacred spaces became confined in enclosed structures that became increasingly more ornate. While this may be seen as a natural outgrowth of sophistication in architecture, it also reflects the belief that humans became separated from the Divine Reality through either ignorance (as asserted in Eastern philosophy) or "original sin" (as depicted in Christianity), and lost their ability to live in accord with Divine Law. The sacred was no longer perceived as part of the natural world. It therefore became necessary to prepare an appropriate, holy and protected place for people to feel connected with the Divine.

Unfortunately, sacred architecture and all its adornments can become a distraction along one's spiritual path if, in the eyes of

---

*   According to Swami Harshananda, built temples did not yet exist during the Vedic age.[2] Also, consider the description of the burnt offering on the altar made after the mythological great flood in the Epic of Gilgamesh and in the book of Genesis (Gen. 8:20, 21).

the devotee, the representational edifice and the objects it contains become more important than the spiritual essence they represent.

Revivals in spirituality, particularly when they are grounded in the experience of spiritual enlightenment, tend to include views that run counter to the notion of sacred adornments and confined sacred space. Buddha's enlightenment took place under the Bodhi tree, not in a sacred temple filled with decorative icons. The Christian book of Acts asserts that "The God who made the world and everything in it ... does not live in shrines made by man, nor is he served by human hands, as though he needed anything" (Acts 17:24, 25).

In the Hindu faith, the Upanishads were written in an effort to shift the attention away from physical representations of the sacred in order to return the emphasis to inner experience; i.e., the realization that the Divine is omnipresent and beyond limits, dwelling everywhere, including within us. Thus from the perspective of the mystical experience, the temple that is closest to us is our own body in which the Spirit of God, the spark or light of divinity within us, dwells. Or as the apostle Paul writes "Do you not know that your body is a temple of the Holy Spirit within you?" (I Cor. 6:19).

In Hinduism, the temple is said to symbolize both the Body of God on a macrocosmic plane, but also the human body on a microcosmic plane. On page 97 is a diagram of the Nataraja Temple in Chidambaram, Tamil Nadu, India. I was astounded when I visited this temple in March of 2000 to find that shrines had been placed at key spots on the temple grounds and designated with names used to refer to parts of the human body, such as the heart, the navel, and the "third eye" which is the eye of insight.

In this chapter, I explore the concept of temple as a metaphor for the reflective, contemplative experience. In addition, I propose ways sacred space can be designed so as to minimize the risk of it becoming a material attachment that retards, rather than advances, one's spiritual growth.

I wander the desert quiet of unknowing,
A nebulaic cloud where fire singes inner space
   and thoughts incubate like sleeping stars.

I peer into the night where epiphanies ring deep,
Igniting mind-filled oceans with thoughts
   that sudden the soul.
There the solar wind winds through light years
   warped by the gravity of human failings.

I seek the wisdom radiating from the edge of the
   silent Self,
Striking the eye with light that propels us to the
   realm of never-ending day.

Listen between breaths and enchanted hymns,
Wait for the Word heard in that pristine dawn
   ages before forms were given names.

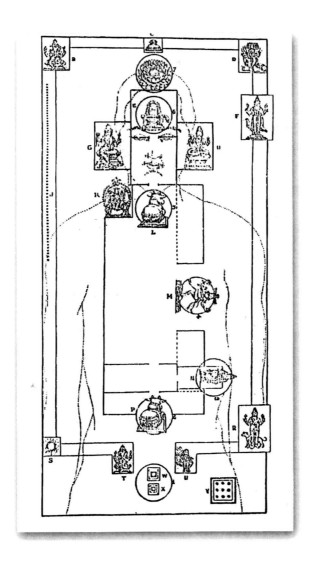

A diagram of the grounds of the Nataraja Temple in Chidambaram,
Tamil Nadu, India

The Inner Sanctuary

One of the most transporting sacred spaces I have entered is the Basilica di Santa Croce (Church of the Holy Cross) in Florence, Italy. I was there in 1992, en route to an international music conference in Pesaro where I had been invited to perform a new composition by Italian-American composer Ernesto Pelligrini. Ernie, as he is called by his friends and colleagues, proudly showed me the treasures of Florence that were born during the height of the Italian Renaissance.

The Basilica di Santa Croce (Church of the Holy Cross)
in Florence, Italy

Michelangelo's tomb in the Basilica di Santa Croce
in Florence, Italy

So what is it that makes space sacred? In my mind, three things: the presence of silence, an atmosphere of humility, and tradition—or what I call the *weight of history*. All three of these qualities lend themselves to putting aside one's ego, which is essential for spiritual growth. The Basilica di Santa Croce imposed a deep silence as I gazed upon the frescos of Giotto di Bondone and the tombs of Galileo and Michelangelo. It was humbling to walk in the footsteps of individuals who transformed Europe and altered the way humanity viewed its relationship to the cosmos.

The sanctuary is that part of any temple where one can touch silence and find refuge from the outside world. And within the "temple of the body" there is an "inner sanctuary" where we can find rest, become absorbed in silence and experience an embryonic love. This embryonic love is the womb experience where all one's needs are met and no tangible thoughts are formed in the mind to which it can become attached. It is a state of non-desire where the mind finds rest within itself.

There are several ways we can enter and experience our own "inner sanctuary." Most of these spiritual practices fall into the category of meditation. Here I am referring to a very specific genre of meditation procedures that enable a person to experience "awareness by itself." This is the unmanifest status of the mind, the source of thought and all mental activity, expressed in the Upanishads as "pure consciousness."

One such method, which comes to us through the medium of music, applies an ancient form of East Indian chanting. Certain Sanskrit texts, set to a tonal melody on the backdrop of a properly configured drone, and listened to or chanted with the eyes closed for the correct length of time, enable a person to effortlessly enter meditation. The Sanskrit text has a "mantric effect," meaning that the sound of each syllable has an influence on the mind and the nervous system that is independent of meaning. The result is an experience of heightened awareness accompanied by a deep state of relaxation. The voluntary and autonomic nervous systems become attuned to one another and the meditation practitioner enjoys a state of inner harmony.

This particular technique I call Gandharva Meditation since it is derived from a musical tradition in India by the same name (see Appendix 1). During the practice of this and other similar forms of meditation, four experiences become apparent that relate to the temple metaphor.

First, there is the experience of inner quietude. The silence deep within the mind comes to the foreground of our experience while mental activity recedes into the background and can even subside altogether. It is a psycho-physiological experience, the wakeful settling of the mind being accompanied by a profound and enjoyable state of relaxation.

Second, one experiences what I refer to as the "state of non-desire." This condition of non-desire is not an exercise in desire repression. Rather, the mind settles into a state of such inner contentment and tranquility that desires simply are no longer present. To use my own analogy, "sitting in the sunlight, we do not find ourselves desiring a candle." It is not that we have to keep ourselves from desiring a candle. The need for a candle simply does not arise in the mind due to the fulfillment provided by the sunlight.

Third, there is the experience of transcendence or "awareness by itself." In mystical literature, awareness is equated with light. It is the basis of experiencing and knowing. In the Upanishads, "pure consciousness" is said to be "beyond thought" yet "not beyond the meditation of the sage."[3] To use the metaphor of a movie, pure consciousness is the "screen" onto which all thought and sensory images, i.e., the "movie," are cast. Conversely, ignorance is customarily equated with darkness. In the Bhagavad Gita, Krishna says, "I destroy the darkness born of ignorance by the shining light of wisdom."[4] And, the Gospel of John quotes Jesus as saying, "he who follows me will not walk in darkness but have the light of life" (John 8:12). In the context of the mystical experience, this "light of life" or "light of wisdom" is that inner pristine awareness which, when experienced by itself, free from desires and the boundaries and limitations of thought, awakens our mental faculties that make possible deep insight. This is the light of our higher spiritual nature, the image of God in which we are created which is the source of epiphany or realization. In the Christian tradition, Quakers are noted for their belief that, in matters of the spirit, following one's "inner light" should supersede or overrule theological law and church doctrine. This teaching dates back to English Quaker George Fox, and to colonial times in the United States where it evolved into the issue of "freedom of conscience." Central to Quaker belief is that people must learn to follow their inner light.

Finally, the meditative experience places the practitioner in a state of inner reflection. In the state of non-desire, the voluntary individual will has been temporarily disengaged and one is left to "witness" the involuntary stream of subtle, non-directed thoughts and feelings flowing within. This involuntary stream of subtle mental activity is the fertile ground of unlimited creative potential from which realizations are spontaneously born. I like to describe it as entering a contemplative state where a person is able to "listen" to one's inner voice. Through the regular practice of meditation one becomes increasingly aware of this wellspring within, and also, more receptive to the realizations that arise from this reservoir of creativity.

Confined sacred spaces such as we have in a temple, church, synagogue or mosque include features that represent the four experiences common to contemplative practice described above. First, regardless of the religious context, we give things that are sacred to us a special place in our lives, separate from mundane worldly life. The Hebrew word for "holy," *Qadosh*, literally means "to be set apart for a special purpose." A sacred space is, therefore, treated with reverence. Rather than fill the space with our own rambling speech, we seek to have the space speak to us. We want it to be a place where we can listen deeply, be receptive to personal insight and hear the voice of Divinity within. Respecting the silence present in the space is an important means of honoring the silence and preserving its sanctity. This silence is conducive to removing sensory distractions and objects of desire so the mind can begin to settle and engage in spiritual practice.

Second, the decor within the space places emphasis on virtue and sacrifice. In doing so, it facilitates the presence of an inward-looking mind settled in the state of non-desire. In ages where the vast majority of the public was illiterate, temple artwork became a means through which the epic stories of heroism, virtue and self-sacrifice, important to a religious tradition, were taught and passed on to succeeding generations. Such stories inspire devotees to realize and be guided by their higher spiritual, selfless nature that is free from egocentric motivations.*

Third, there is a noticeable light source, a strategically placed window or flame, symbolizing the power the light of realization has over the darkness of ignorance.

Finally, any rituals that take place in the sacred space, whether they be in the form of personal devotions or group ceremonies, carry rich symbolic meaning revealed as one reflects on the imagery within the ceremonial rites and, where permitted, in the temple artwork.

While a sacred space contains features that facilitate meditative practice, from the perspective of mysticism and the experience of spiritual enlightenment, the outer temple is but a pale reflection of our unbounded inner space. When probed by the insightful mind, this inner space is far more meaningful than finite representations of attributes set within the built environment. In the opening pages of the final chapter of his masterpiece *Walden*, Henry David Thoreau offers a nineteenth century reflection on the boundless experience of inner space. He challenges us to "be a Columbus to whole new

---

*   An exception is the sculptures that adorn many Hindu temples in India which Westerners might consider erotic. Such sculptures are thought to be a test for the devotee; i.e., if you are aroused by the artworks your mind is not pure enough to enter the temple. Swami Harshananda explains them as connected to fertility rites, and as representations of the bipolar nature of the created world wherein nature (prakriti) and spirit (purusha) are united.[5]

worlds and continents within you, opening new channels, not of trade, but of thought," and to "explore the private seas, the Atlantic and Pacific oceans of one's being alone."[6]

Once a person is awakened through the meditative experience, a growth process begins whereby one starts to internalize the meaning within scripture and within ceremonies in a way that validates inner experience. In Indian Philosophy, this process of internalization becomes important in the third stage of life known as *vanaprastha*.* In this stage, a person has become a forest dweller, and one's spiritual practice consists of meditation and symbolic worship rather than participation in temple rituals. In addition, the fourth and final stage of life in Indian Philosophy is known as *sannyasa*. The aspirant in this stage lives free from worldly attachments and becomes engaged in the uninterrupted contemplation of Brahman, the Ultimate Reality. According to Swami Nikhilananda, for a sannyasin:

> It was no longer necessary to worship God by means of material articles or even mental symbols. One experienced directly the non-duality of God, the soul, and the universe—Spirit communing immediately with Spirit. The Sannyasin took the vow of dedicating his life to Truth and to the service of humanity, and was honored as a spiritual leader of society. And it was for him that the Upanishads ... were written.[7]

The Upanishads are a series of texts included in the sixth system of Indian philosophy known as Vedanta. Their focus is primarily on the experience of spiritual enlightenment—understanding

* The first two stages of life in Indian Philosophy are brahmacharya, when one is a student, and garhasthya, when a person becomes a householder.[8]

Brahman not as a theoretical construct but through direct experience, and realizing the forces of nature not as objects of worship but as expressions of the universal Supreme Self. But the process of internalizing religious precepts to validate inner experience is not restricted to Hinduism. It is found in all the major religious traditions and is strikingly apparent in writings of the apostle Paul.

For example, Paul internalizes the veil in the Jewish temple when he describes the "veil" that lies over the minds of those hearing the words of Moses (II Cor. 3:15). Paul also uses the crucifixion as a metaphor for the sacrifice of his own lower, egocentric nature that is bound by the law, saying that he has been "crucified with Christ; it is no longer I who live, but Christ who lives in me" (Gal. 2:20). By internalizing the rituals, one understands their meaning as metaphors as they relate to a person's own religious tradition and individualized personal growth.

The following experience, which I had while hiking in the Blue Ridge Mountains in Virginia, is one of many which have led me to emphasize the inner temple as we all proceed on our individual spiritual journeys.

> Amidst graceful pines and struggling wildflowers there is a shrine atop a steep sloping hill. I go there to make offerings on its sacrificial altar. To begin, I offer the sacrifice of time, then the dimensions of space—of height, breadth and width. Next comes the offering of speech, followed by breath, individual will, ego and craving. Lastly I lay down the sacrifice of thought.
>
> This shrine, with its majestic canopy is not made of stone or with human hands. There are no lighted candles, no sticks of burning incense, and no choirs intoning hymns. It is suspended in pure light, heated by boundless love, enveloped in the harmony of the subtlest impulses, fluctuating in pure wakefulness, radiating from within, expanding

endlessly. Those who seek earnestly and can enter this
inner shrine, hear the Divine voice in their native tongue.
Its meaning dawns like a newborn star. There is no need
for translation.

The process of internalization also gives the rituals and stories
more personal meaning and a validity that transcends their historical context. One can then appreciate the stories more for their
mythological meaning. By mythological meaning, I refer to that
meaning inherent to a story that is valid irrespective of whether or
not the story is historically true. As I explain in Chapter 2, myth
transcends time and place and speaks to us on a deep intuitive level,
revealing to us something about our own psychological and sometimes physiological nature. When we extract mythological meaning,
the events, persons, or objects a story contains are recognized to be
metaphors for attributes that comprise our own subjective nature.

Two meaningful examples of stories that pertain to the temple
metaphor, to be considered for their mythological and internalized
meaning, are found in the Christian and Jewish traditions. The
first is the account of Jesus chasing the moneychangers out of the
temple in Jerusalem which I already described in Chapter 2 (see
the subtitled section "Knowledge Revealed from Within"). Interpreted as allegory, this story becomes a parable that speaks to the
purifying experience of meditation. The temple is the body, filled
with selfish desires and cravings for the material world (as symbolized by the moneychangers), which is cleansed by the "light of life
within." For the Christian, this light is the *Inner Christ*, recognized
through meditation to awaken us to more profound realizations
and wisdom. Each time one sits to meditate, the moneychangers
are cast out of one's own bodily temple as the mind settles into a
state of inner tranquility and contentment.

A comparable symbolic message can be found in the Hanukkah
story from the Jewish tradition. Historically speaking, in 168 BCE,

the Jewish temple in Jerusalem was taken over by Syrian and Greek soldiers. The temple was used to worship Zeus, as the emperor Antiochus had outlawed the practice of Jewish rituals. The Jews eventually rebelled in what has become romanticized as the first battle ever fought for religious freedom. These Jewish rebels became known as the Maccabees.

The word Hanukkah means "dedication" and refers to the rededication of the Jewish temple after it had been defiled by the Syrian-Greek takeover. Purification of the temple required the burning of the lamp in the temple for eight days. But there was only enough oil for the lamp to remain lit for one day. Those in charge of the temple went out seeking oil to complete the rededication, but when they returned, miraculously, they found the lamp still burning.

Interpreted as myth, the temple in the Hanukkah story becomes the body, the temple of the soul. The light in our bodily temple is experienced as the inner light of realization. As a person meditates over time, it is recognized that this inner light is eternally present and continues to burn, regardless of the battles we may be waging in life outside the temple of the body.

For the Jewish mystic, this inner light becomes the source of the Hasidic masters' passionate, ecstatic, and transforming love. As Andrew Harvey expresses in his foreword to a book of Hasidic tales, "This bliss-fire of Divine love, underpins the whole of the universe and is boundless like the heart it streams from forever."[9]

Christian mystic Saint John of the Cross uses similar language to describe his experience of what he calls the "living flame of love" that purifies and transforms the soul.

> This flame the soul feels within it, not only as a fire that has consumed and transformed it in sweet love, but also as a fire that burns within it and sends out flame, as I have said, and that flame bathes the soul in glory and refreshes it with the temper of Divine life.[10]

Through such a transformative experience, the veil of ignorance is removed and the mind of the devotee is illumined, leaving the faculties of realization fully receptive and awake.*

Designing Sacred Spaces

The internalization of religious stories and teachings is of utmost importance in a person's spiritual journey. When we appreciate the mythological dimension of religion, we are able to extract its timeless, cross-cultural and universal meaning; timeless in that the meaning appeals to many generations and is valid independent of historical accuracy, cross-cultural in that the symbols used are shared between cultures, and universal in that it speaks to our innate human nature at a depth that transcends our ethnic background or personal worldview.

The problem with built temples is that they can, in all their grandeur, be a distraction from the inner essence of the spiritual experience and risk misleading the devotee into thinking that Truth is to be found in dogma, design, icons and geographical location. Given what we know about the universe today, we should realize that the earth is light-years away from any other inhabitable planet. From this perspective, our entire planet is a sacred space.

While specific lands or architectural structures may carry special personal or historical meaning, we must not lose sight of the natural beauty and rich diversity of life our planet harbors. The belief that there are geographical "holy lands" unique to any of the world

---

* Veils were part of ancient Jewish temples where one was used to shroud the entrance to the most holy part of the shrine. Indian Philosophy speaks of the "veil of maya" (maya meaning literally "that which is not") which shrouds the soul leaving one in ignorance.

religions diminishes the sacred status we should attribute to the entire earth. Our planetary residence is a remote sacred temple of life in our Milky Way galaxy, isolated by light years of desolate space.

One might therefore find it somewhat rebellious, that in a chapter on how we define and design sacred space, I would be advocating no geographical location and no design at all! There is, however, a role for designated sacred gathering places if they are built to call attention to the spiritual dimension of life, initially experienced by looking within.

Spirituality unfolds through a growth process that begins in infancy. As we mature spiritually, the teachings and myths of the great world religions are meant to be appreciated on different levels of meaning. Literal interpretation is then recognized to be either historically inaccurate or superficial. In addition, the meaning apparent to a long time adult devotee may not be the meaning appropriate for a child. As an example, let us consider the well-known Christian nativity story.

For a person who has spent time reading and reflecting on the theological underpinnings of the concept of incarnation, the virgin birth becomes a metaphor for the principle of the "Prime Mover" or *First Cause*. That is, the birth is not the result of the chain of cause and effect, but occurs as a direct intervention from the Divine. Incarnation articulates the mystery of how the Divine manifests within each of us without anticipation through the process of realization, which is the experience of epiphany. These realizations are experienced as direct and intuitive; they are not arrived at through inquiry or a step-by-step logical thought process.

At another stage, the nativity of Christ becomes understood for its Zen-like teaching of value inversion. The supreme omnipotent Creator of the universe enters his own creation in the humblest and simplest of circumstances, with the announcement of the birth given to those who were among the lowest in the social order of the day, the shepherds. For devotees who hold to a literal interpretation, the nativity may be understood primarily as an incomprehensible miracle, while for a sexually un-awakened child, it is a story of idealizing motherhood and birth, and depicting the wonder and simplicity of the Divine gift as it occurs within the cold, unwelcome domain of the physical world.

As a father of two children, I could observe and assist my children as they progress through some of the stages I have mentioned. Unfortunately, many of the established religions, and here I include the popular expressions of all faiths, do not adequately guide a person towards appreciating the internalized, mythological meaning of scripture.

One way to address this deficiency is to design sacred space so as to depict multiple interpretations of the stories important to a given religious tradition. Temple art and design could juxtapose different interpretations so as to encourage believers to view religion more holistically. They could also encourage the process of internalization of religious teachings.

A second approach to encourage a broader view of religion is to employ design to call attention to stories, themes, and metaphors that the great world religions share in common. Today, there is a very active interfaith movement spreading in the United States and throughout the world. International organizations such as the United Religions Initiative (URI) are gaining in social influence and are having a positive impact. It is quite possible that, in the near future, architects will be called upon to design interfaith spaces of worship. Successful designs could help counter the provincialism inherent to popular religion.

For example, in addition to the Christian nativity story, there are several other miraculous birth images present in the various religious traditions. In Greek mythology, it was Athena, the goddess of wisdom, who was born from the head of Zeus. This image is admittedly a somewhat crude way of expressing the experience of a sudden realization, and is perhaps still with us in our language today when we speak of a realization as being "mind-blowing." The Jewish story of Sarah, a woman with a "barren womb" who miraculously gives birth to Isaac in her old age, teaches us that age is no barrier to the transforming power that lies within the realm of human potential.

How many times has it been said that infants must crawl before they can walk, a process that also has symbolized human development from a selfish animal nature (walking on four legs as a quadruped) to a mature moral awareness and selfless stage of living?

A miraculous birth image in popular Buddhist culture describes Buddha as being born from the side of his mother and immediately walking upright, suggesting that Buddha was not born with a selfish animal nature. Such myths, when studied in parallel for their internalized meaning, provide a more complete picture of how ancient writers viewed the human psyche.

The same cross-cultural approach can be taken to teach the myth of the great flood as found in the Epic of Gilgamesh, the myth of Prometheus, and in the Vishnu Prana, as well as in the story of Noah and the Ark in the book of Genesis. People should also be aware that the teaching of death and renewal is represented in the myth of the phoenix, the story of Nachiketa in the Katha Upanishad, as well as in the death and resurrection of Christ in the gospels.

Stories about consuming sacred food speak directly to the importance of internalizing religious teachings, because when food is eaten, it becomes part of one's body, absorbed into one's being. The soma sacrifice in the Rig Veda, as explained previously in Chapter 4, the manna given to the Israelites during their 40 years in the wilderness, the Zoroastrian drink of immortality, the well-known Christian communion rite, the story in the Mahabharata of Krishna dispelling the hunger of Durvasa and his 10,000 disciples,[11] and Jesus feeding the multitude of 5,000 people, are all examples of the sacred food metaphor.* In addition, the elimination of thirst as a metaphor for life without craving is found in the Chandogya Upanishad,[12] the teachings of Buddha (Nirvana is also known by the term "tanhakkayha" which means "extinction of thirst"),[13] and in the Gospel of John where Jesus says: "He who drinks the water I shall give him shall never thirst" (John 4:13).

A third approach to challenge people to consider inventive interpretations is to design temples, mosques and churches with the intent of reconnecting us with the natural world, and encouraging the integration of science into theology. Envision, for example, a sacred shrine devoted to the infinite Divine creative power at work in the universe. Rather than having a mural depicting the destruction of Sodom and Gomorrah, there could be a wall-size photo of a supernova; rather than God separating the light from the darkness, a gaseous nebula as viewed by the Hubble Space Telescope wherein lies the birthplace of stars; rather than the rainbow arching across the sky after the great flood, a photo of the aurora borealis gracing the northern sky could be displayed. Architects should also consider temporarily projecting some of the images I have described as a way for reminding the temple visitor that nothing in this physical world, and indeed in the entire universe, is permanent.

It would be impractical of course, and certainly undesirable, to cram all these themes into one piece of sacred architecture. However,

---

* The story of Christ feeding the multitude is in all four gospels, but it actually occurs twice in Matthew. The first account (Matt. 14:14–21) the number for the crowd is 5000 men; the second time (Matt. 15:32–39) the number given is 4000. But in each rendition, after giving the number, it says "besides women and children." Assuming many of the men in the audience had their wife present, and perhaps children as well, that easily brings the number up to 10,000, the same figure that is found in the Mahabharata. The meaning often given to the story in the Mahabharata is that simply the presence of the Lord is all that is necessary to dispel hunger and fulfill all desires.

a focused theme can be addressed in any given design. In ancient times, temples were dedicated to a particular god or goddess, or a medieval church honored a particular saint. Likewise, sacred space in our new millennium could focus on multiple interpretations of a specific religious concept or story, a shared interreligious theme or value, or on drawing upon science and the natural world to gain insight into our selfless, altruistic spiritual nature.

Clapping with One Hand

Architects, painters, sculptors and musicians, by means of the artworks they have created, have had a great deal of influence on the development of popular religion.* It is important though, that artists and designers guard against having a material representation of a religious concept become a distraction from the spiritual essence the artistic or architectural design represents. For as sacred representations become more developed and complex, there is a great risk of attachment. An example of great beauty and complexity

---

*   Oftentimes, works of art contribute to inaccuracy or misrepresentation in popular religion. It became common, for example, in Christian nativity paintings, for artists to depict three magi or wise men as visiting the Christ child in the stable where he was born. The Gospel of Matthew, however, does not stipulate how many Magi there were. It only says that the Magi brought three gifts, these being gold, frankincense and myrrh. In addition, Matthew's gospel says the Magi entered the "house" where the family was, not the stable. Jesus would have been a toddler when the Magi arrived, as it would have taken between one and two years for them to make the trip from Persia to Bethlehem. For this reason, Herod, the King of Judea at the time, orders the slaughter of all male children in Bethlehem who were under two years of age (see Matthew 2: 16).

in Tibetan Buddhism is the sand mandala created as a spiritual exercise by Tibetan monks. But to minimize the risk of attachment to the outer form, the mandala is destroyed shortly after completion. This is what we metaphorically must do everyday with our temples.

Meditation is a means of destroying ego attachment within the temple of the body. When experiencing transcendence or "awareness by itself," all thought and individuality are dissolved and become unmanifest in preparation for its renewal as we arise from meditation and begin activity. Or to use the temple analogy attributed to Jesus in the Christian gospels, we must "destroy our temple" and raise it up again (John 2:19–21). This is the ongoing process of death and renewal we witness day after day in creation and within us, transforming our consciousness until duality dissolves, and we recognize the inner and the outer as one (see the Gospel of Thomas, Verse 22). Then we come to know what in Zen Buddhist philosophy is referred to as "the sound of one hand clapping"—the Creator applauding to express the joy that comes when oneness is realized by the earnest seeker. And because God is beyond duality, God only has one hand to clap with.*

---

*   The "sound of one hand clapping" in Zen Buddhism is comparable to the concept of the "unstruck sound" in Indian Philosophy. When one hand claps, there is nothing for it to strike against. The "unstruck sound" is a metaphor for the primal wave or vibration arising on the "ocean" of the Unmanifest in preparation for bringing forth Creation. Because the unmanifest field is infinite, nothing can come from outside the field to strike it to initiate the vibration; i.e., there is no "outside" to infinity. Thus, the primal wave must arise from within itself by virtue of its own nature to manifest.

CHAPTER 6

The Mystery of Oneness

The aspect of the world that we ordinarily perceive is that of isolated parts. ... To us, things do seem disconnected and unrelated. Yet this is an illusion and a distortion of the underlying behind-the-scene oneness and unity, which is an intrinsic quality of the world. ...

Our greatest spiritual achievement may lie in total integration of the spiritual and the physical—in realizing that the spiritual and the physical are not two aspects of ourselves, but one.

—Larry Dossey, MD
Space, Time and Medicine

I have always been a person in search of threads—threads that bind together diverse ideas, threads that reunite friends and family members who have become estranged, threads that make up the fabric of reconciliation, threads that weave the many into one.

In the year 2000, I made my second pilgrimage to India. My first pilgrimage was to study Hindustani music; this time it was to lecture and perform at Annamalai University in the exotic temple town of Chidambaram in the southern state of Tamil Nadu. I was a professor leading an international field-trip experience for a group of students from the Ball State University School of Music. Some members of the group had never ventured beyond the borders of the United States. One student in particular came from a family of tobacco farmers in Kentucky. For him, the experience of an American university, let alone being immersed in a land as culturally rich and foreign as India, was a pilgrimage. As I told my students before we boarded our flight, visiting India is like being on another planet.

One cannot, and certainly should not, go to India to specialize in one discipline of study. The social climate of India is inherently integrated with a consciousness of connectedness. In fact, an underlying principle at the heart of Indian philosophy is that of *Adviata,* which means "all is one" (literally: "not two"). Adviata is both a concept and an intimate awareness; an explanation for the experience of unity consciousness where oneness is perceived and known to be the ultimate and essential Reality underlying and pervading creation. Henry David Thoreau refers to this ultimate and essential Reality in his book *A Week on the Concord and Merrimack Rivers,* when he writes of "that everlasting something to which we are all allied."[1] Ralph Waldo Emerson calls it the *oversoul,* which he further describes as "indefinable and unmeasurable,"[2] yet intimately a part of us as it is "... that Unity ... within which every Man's particular being is contained and made one with all other ..."[3]*

Adviata philosophy is embodied in the ancient approach to education in India, where music, linguistics, mathematics, astronomy, poetry, dance, and philosophy are studied simultaneously, woven together in a profound relational cultural equation of creative thought. The Mundaka Upanishad declares that there are two kinds of knowledge, the higher and the lower. The lower is the knowledge of the Vedas, and also of the customary academic disciplines. The higher knowledge is that by which "one comes to know the changeless reality." It is this higher knowledge which reveals "that which transcends the senses, that which is uncaused, which is

---

* Emerson was well versed in Indian philosophy. His concept of "oversoul" is virtually identical to the Hindu Brahman, which is often referred to in the Upanishads as the Supreme Self and Ultimate Reality to be realized by the earnest seeker of Truth.

indefinable … which is all pervading, subtler that the subtest—the everlasting source of all."[4] In such a cultural context, the Western approach to higher education, with its emphasis on reductionist specialization, seems strikingly out of place.

This Adviata view is expounded in Vedanta, the sixth and culminating system of Indian Philosophy. And one place in South India where it is uniquely represented and expressed is at Shantivanam, a monastery near Tiruchirapalli in Tamil Nadu. Shantivanam is affiliated with the Roman Catholic Church and is known as a Benedictine Indian Rite Monastery that offers a unique interfaith experience while remaining within the Roman Catholic tradition. Since my second pilgrimage to India took me to the Tamil Nadu region, I wanted to take my students to Shantivanam to experience the ambience of this sacred place. I was also interested in meeting Brother John Martin, an Indian Christian monastic residing at Shantivanam whose writings on the *beatitudes* had impressed me deeply. Our hosts at Annamalai University graciously agreed to accommodate my wishes.

We departed at 7 AM on a March spring morning. After a three-hour drive through many villages and a varied agrarian landscape, we arrived at the monastery, which our hosts referred to as an ashram. The gate of the monastery features a structure that, from a distance, resembles the architecture of temples in India. Sculptured onto its roof were animals, as is common on Hindu temples. But these animals were those traditionally associated with the four apostles who wrote the gospels. On one corner was a lion, the animal associated with Saint Mark. On another, an ox, which symbolizes Saint Luke. On the opposite corners were positioned a man, associated with Matthew, and the eagle which represents Saint John.*

---

*   These animals can also be seen adorning the top of St. Marks Cathedral in Venice.

As we entered the grounds of the ashram, I saw a solitary figure walking along a path wearing a loincloth. I immediately recognized him as Brother John Martin. His smile and darshan* was radiant and exuded the joy of a renunciant devoted to God realization. He seemed to know that we had made a long trip as he welcomed us with delight. After he passed us by, we walked further into the grounds and were told that we were invited to have lunch with the other residents after the 11:30 AM interfaith prayer service.

The prayer service was held in an open covered structure as is common in southern India. It began with several readings representing the major religions that have flourished in India. Those from the Bible and the Qur'an were read, while those taken from the Vedas and Buddhist scripture were chanted. The readings were followed by a period of silent meditation which closed with the Lord's Prayer. The entire service then concluded with a ritual known in Hindu worship as an *arti*. A tray which held burning camphor was passed before a covered box, open on the front side, illuminating the religious icon. The camphor melts as it burns symbolizing the melting of the heart and the surrendering of the ego. In a Hindu ritual, the icon would be an image of Shiva or other Hindu deity. In this Christianized ritual, the icon was the Cross.

Father Jules Monchanin (1895–1957) and Dom Henri La Saux (1910–1973) founded Shantivanam in 1950. Both were interested in pursuing a Christian-Vedanta dialog. They considered themselves Christian "sannyasi" which is the term used to refer to a Hindu monk.[†] Fr. Monchanin adopted the name of Swami Parama Arupi Ananda and Henri Le Saux became known as Swami Abishiktananda. In 1968, Shantivanam came under the direction of the Benedictine monk Father Bede Griffiths who lived until 1993.

---

* Darshan: an Indian term for the presence one feels when in the company of someone auspicious.

[†] See Chapter 5, page 104 for an explanation of the related term "sannyasa," which in Indian Philosophy is the fourth and final stage of life.

As a point of departure, the concept of Adviata or oneness is alluded to in the Gospel of John where Jesus, in his final prayer before being arrested in the Garden of Gethsemane, is quoted as asking, "...that they [his disciples] may all be one; even as thou, Father, art in me, and I in thee, that they also may be in us ..." (John 17:21). Furthermore, the intent of the Christian communion ritual is that Christ "may dwell in us and we in Him." A similar passage is found in the Hindu scripture, the Bhagavad Gita, where Lord Krishna says: "those who worship Me with devotion, they are in Me and I am in them" (Ch. 9:29).[5]

There are also remarkably similar verses found in Hindu and Christian scriptures that speak to the inherent omnipresence of the Divine. Compare, for example, the following verses found respectively in the Upanishads and the Christian book of Acts:

> The whole Universe came forth from Brahman and moves in Brahman. ... In Brahman it lives and has its being. (The Katha Upanishad)[6]

> "Yet God is not far from each of us. For in God we live and move and have our being." (Acts 17:27, 28)

How do we understand such passages? How do we understand the way in which we, as individual human beings, can become one with the living, infinite, Divine Presence Fr. Thomas Keating refers to as Ultimate Mystery? How can we understand the idea that things can be different and yet one at the same time? How are we to understand what the mystics meant when they spoke of becoming "one with God?"

I maintain that we cannot fully intellectually understand such mysteries. Nor can we speak of them accurately with objective or scientific language. Their experience is ineffable, beyond what words can express. We can however, appreciate the experience and make use of parables and paradoxical language, as well as analogies and metaphors drawn from science, to help us gain this appreciation.

The Gate to Shantivanam, Benedictene monastery
in the Tiruchirapalli district of Tamil Nadu, India

The experience of Shantivanam cannot be fully appreciated at the time of one's visit. But the experience leaves impressions of serenity and wholeness embedded deep within the mind. Over time, these impressions are processed by the subconscious and eventually germinate, manifesting as epiphanies and insights that provide one with a more profound understanding of life and the illusory nature of the universe in which we live. The result is a more spiritually mature human being, whole in one's self-identity, as embodied in Brother John Martin.

The environment of Shantivanam is a source of positive spiritual energy that facilitates the experience of oneness. The students who accompanied me there sensed the peace and serenity of the ashram, and, like me, could not help but take at least a portion of this serenity with them.

Metaphors for Oneness Drawn from Science and Art

Several of the world religions have expressions for the indwelling Divine nature. Hindu sages have long said that we all have the "spark of divinity" within us. Buddhists say we all have "Buddha nature." The phrase that comes from Judaism and Christianity, that humans are "created in the image of God," is perhaps the most familiar expression for Westerners.

How can we come to understand the paradoxical notion that each of us is dwelling in God and, at the same time, God is dwelling in us? Or as it says in the Katha Upanishad, "What is within us is also without. What is without is also within."[7] How can the macrocosm be found within the microcosm?

Expressed in the language of mathematics, this is like saying that set A is a subset of set B, yet at the same time, set B is also a subset of set A. If sets A and B are not equal, then such as relationship is impossible.

The Creator placing himself in his own creation has been alluded to by painters, poets and composers who cryptically place themselves in their own creative work. Filippino Lippi, in his painting *Martyrdom of Saint Peter,* places himself in the painting as an onlooker. In his poem "A Hymn to God the Father," John Donne closes each stanza with a trope using his name: "When Thou has done, Thou hast not done." And Johann Sebastian Bach encoded his name in several of his compositions with the famous BACH motif.*

An example from modern science that helps explain this paradox of the macrocosm embedded in microcosm is that of the hologram. If I take a typical photographic negative and cut it up into several pieces, the image on the negative becomes fragmented. The whole is lost. But if I slice up a holographic negative, the entire image is preserved. That's because in a hologram, every part contains the complete image (albeit from a slightly different perspective). Analogously, in humans, every cell contains the complete genetic profile of that person. In terms of genetic information, each part contains the whole. A dwells within B, and B also dwells within A.

From the discovery of holography has also come a new way of looking at the universe called the holographic paradigm. It is a concept developed by quantum field theorist David Bohm who was an associate of Albert Einstein. This view suggests that the material reality we perceive is some form of projection, much like a holographic image is projected when laser light passes through a holographic negative of interfering wave patterns.

At the micro level, matter essentially consists of waves of energy. These waves form patterns much like ripples created by two different disturbances on the surface of a pond that intersect and interfere

---

* The BACH motif in German is comprised of the pitches B-flat, A, C, and B natural.

with one another. Bohm goes so far as to say that what we call the universe is actually a "holoverse." This holoverse is a projection of coherent energy waves much like a projected holographic image is comprised of coherent, standing waves of light. Bohm further suggests that this holographic analogy should not be thought of only as involving the medium of visible light. All waves of energy interfering with one another potentially create the holographic reality in which we live. One could say that we ourselves are a kind of projection, like a holographic image, of the universal consciousness as it passes through the interference pattern that encodes the deepest level of our individuality.[8]

Again, using the hologram as a metaphor, it is as if we are all grounded in a field of interference patterns. Our roots, so to speak, extend into this field, where the coordinates and reference points we normally use to navigate through life do not exist. In this field, the dimensions of time and space are not as we experience them in the projected illusion of the material universe. Physicist Leonard Susskind, in collaboration with his colleague Gerard 't Hooft, describes it as follows in Chapter 18 of his book *The Black Hole War*:

> The three-dimensional world of ordinary experience—the universe filled with galaxies, stars, planets, houses, boulders and people—is a hologram, an image of reality coded on a distant two-dimensional surface. This new law of physics, known as the Holographic Principle, asserts that everything inside a region of space can be described by bits of information restricted to the boundary.[9]

And later in Chapter 24, Susskind somewhat reluctantly admits "that the solid three-dimensional world is an illusion of a sort."[10]

This holographic analogy helps explain how a subatomic particle, like an electron, can be both localized and everywhere at the same time. That is, in quantum reality, the information that defines the electron is "everywhere" in much the same way the information that encodes a holographic image is present throughout the entire holographic negative. It is as if underlying our experience of three-dimensional space is a strange realm of interference patterns like what we find on a holographic negative, with the exception that these interfering "quantum waves" are not frozen but are continuously interacting. In this way the electron "fills the universe" on the quantum level since space and time in the subatomic "realm" operate much differently than how we experience these dimensions in the illusory physical world in which we spend our daily lives.

Another more tangible metaphor for unity among differences is the common experience of matter having three states. We experience water, for example, as having three distinct forms: solid, liquid and gas. If we didn't know better, we might mistakenly conclude that what we are experiencing with our senses are three different substances. Yet we know that on the molecular level, the "substances" we are experiencing are actually one, that is, water in three different forms. The chemical formula, H_2O remains the same, despite what our senses may be telling us.

This metaphor of the three states of matter has been used to explain the concept of Trinity in Christianity, often depicted as three interlocking rings symbolizing eternity, with a common center. The Christian monotheistic concept of God is conceived of as consisting of one essence, yet as assuming three forms. In referring to this I am not arguing either for or against the doctrine of the Trinity as taught in orthodox Christianity. I am merely suggesting this concept of Trinity is still useful as a device to challenge the contemplative mind to entertain the idea that things can be one and yet different at the same time.

Hindu commentators take this idea of "one substance yet different forms" much further. Rather than oneness being found only in a triune Godhead, the sage of India who authored the Chandogya Upanishad perceived the entire material universe as consisting of one substance, much like clay can be used to fashion many different forms, yet still remain in its essence, clay.

> As by knowing one lump of clay, all things of clay are known, the difference being only in name arising from speech, and the truth being that all are clay ... exactly so is that knowledge, knowing which we know all.[11]

Interlocking rings as a symbol for the Christian Trinity—
Eternity and oneness represented in one image

From the point of view of Indian philosophy, all things share a common or universal "essence." One might initially think of this as an over-generalization, yet today, quantum physics and the theory of relativity tell us that the entire material universe can be conceived of as energy being expressed in different forms. Ultimately, everything is energy.

A geometric model for oneness can be found in what is called the Möbius strip. August Ferdinand Möbius was a German mathematician for whom this three-dimensional geometric form

was named.* To form a Möbius strip, you take a strip of paper, give
one end a half twist, then connect the two ends so that the strip of
paper has a continuous surface. When thus connected, the strip of
paper, which originally had two sides and two edges, now is found
to have only one side and one edge or boundary.

Conceptually, the Möbius strip is a metaphor for two differing
perspectives within which one can view a conflict. If we see only
a portion of the strip, it appears to have two opposing sides. But
a holistic view of the form reveals that what appears as two sides
is actually one. The opposition one perceives merely results from
seeing only a fragment of the strip.

If we apply this conceptualization to the seasons of fall and spring
within the yearly cycle, for example, fall and spring appear to be
in conflict. In the fall living things appear to die, and in the spring
they are born. But the success of the spring season is dependent
on the success of the fall, and the success of the fall depends on
the success of the spring. Both seasons exist on a complementary
continuum as they flow through summer and winter from one into
the other. Both rely on each other for their coexistence. So too, if
our awareness, and therefore our knowledge, is acquired from a
limited perspective, we perceive opposition and conflict. But if our
awareness is holistic, we see common ground and the potential for
a cooperative and mutually beneficial relationship.

This is not to say that the conflicts we experience are not real,
only that we often create our own conflicts by losing sight of the
big picture. Conflicts can also have a positive side if we are able to
"stand back" and see them as providing opportunities for understanding, opening up conversations that deepen our relationships.

---

*   Both August Ferdinand Möbius and Johann Benedict Listing are
credited with independently discovering this geometric form in 1858.

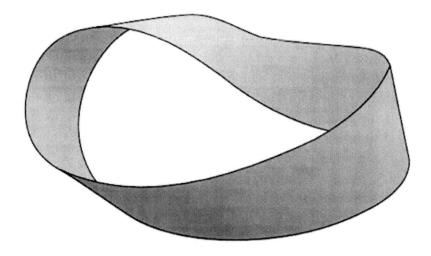

Möbius strip—a three-dimensional form
with one side and one edge

Forgiveness and Quantum Reality

Anyone trying to get their neural networks around Albert Einstein's theory of relativity has to entertain the question of how an object can be both at rest and in motion at the same time. Or, expressed philosophically, how can moving and not moving be one?

The very act of entertaining this question is a break from the way Isaac Newton perceived the world. For Newton, time was a constant, and space was kind of absolute grid from which all motion can be measured. They are distinctly separate concepts. An object in motion stays in motion until an external force acts upon it. But for

Einstein, time and space are united in a continuum that is relative rather than absolute. Why? Because in the context of infinite space, there is no ultimate or permanently stable reference point, either in time or space, from which to view an object. For an object that is in motion, there is a vantage point from which that same object can be said to be at rest; and for every object that is at rest, there is a vantage point from which that object can be said to be in motion.

In the quantum reality, the relativity of motion and its movement forward or backwards can also be applied to time since time and space are thought of on that level as a unified continuum, i.e. "space-time." Nobel Prize-winning physicist Richard Feynman showed how, in certain cases, it is valid to reverse our assessment of subatomic particle interactions and view particles as moving backwards, as well as forwards, in time.[12] His illustrations are expressed in what have become as known as "Feynman diagrams."*

Leonard Susskind's and Gerard 't Hooft's conclusion mentioned earlier, that "the universe ... is a hologram," considered together with Feynman's research, suggests that at the quantum level, the dimensions of time and space are unexpressed in the quantum field of interference patterns. Reality begins to look more like Walt Whitman described it, as a "vast similitude" that "interlocks all," uniting "all of the past, present, future," and "all distances of place, however wide" and "all distances of time."† We are left contemplating the idea that the present moment is all that is.

This realization has profound theological implications when it comes to the concepts of nonattachment and forgiveness. One reads,

---

*   For a layman's explanation of Feynman diagrams in the context of space-time, see *The Tao of Physics* by Fritjof Capra, Boulder: Shambala Publications, 1983, pages 183–184.

†   From a poem by Walt Whitman entitled: "On the Beach at Night Alone."

for example, a great deal about nonattachment in Hindu scripture, particularly in the Bhagavad Gita.

> Having abandoned attachment to the fruits of action, always content and independent, he does nothing even though he is engaged in action. (Bhagavad Gita: 4:20)[13]

> The action of a man who is rid of attachment, who is liberated, whose mind is firmly established in knowledge, who performs action as a sacrifice, is completely dissolved. (Bhagavad Gita: 4:23)[14]

Years ago, when I began studying the Bhagavad Gita, the idea of nonattachment was new to me. As a teaching, I saw it as having no parallel in my own Christian tradition. In the gospels, the words attachment and nonattachment are never used. Years later, I spent a weekend visiting a Christian retreat center where the theme the leaders focused on was forgiveness. They explained forgiveness as a process of "letting go," relinquishing the burden of judgment. It was presented, not as a disciplined obligation dictated by scripture, but as a means through which a person could be freed from the burden of the grudge. After all, if we do not forgive someone who has wronged us, that person still has power over us, shaping our thoughts and casting a shadow over our moods. Suddenly, I saw there was a relationship between the act of forgiving and nonattachment. In fact, I now maintain that forgiveness is the highest form of nonattachment as it frees us from resentment and the gripping desire for revenge.

The past is also illusory in part because it is based on memory. Without memory there would be no concept of past. On the microphysical level, we are actually grounded in the field of interference patterns and the quantum reality. There, time is a variable, not an ontological constant as we mistakenly perceive it to be in our daily experience. Similarly, what we call the future never exists for us because, when it does, it is the present. For each of us, only the present moment is reality.*

To hold a grudge or not forgive, we must assume there is a past. Indeed to hold hate in one's heart, one must erroneously believe in the illusion of the past. Not forgiving is based on non-reality. Forgiveness then becomes a means of breaking one's attachment to this self-constructed illusion we call the past.

Yoga and the Experience of Oneness

In addition to Adviata philosophy, and also to science, techniques ascribed to the system of yoga, which is the fourth system of Indian philosophy, provide insight into the concept of oneness. Yoga is the spiritual practice through which a person gains union with the Divine Presence through direct experience. According to philosophy professor Eliot Deutsch, the word may have been derived from the Sanskrit root *yuj* meaning to "yoke" or "harness," suggesting the act of "joining" or "uniting oneself with."[15] Meditative practices such as Gandharva Meditation (see Appendix 1), that are a part of the yoga system of self-development, settle the mind into a condition of wakeful inner silence and result in a profound state of physical

---

* It turns out that, in addition to the quantum level, time is also a variable in the material reality that is our daily experience. Einstein's theory of special relativity explains how time moves more slowly as a person accelerates relative to the speed of light. Furthermore his theory of general relativity explains that time is affected by the influence of gravitational fields; i.e., the stronger the gravitational field, the slower time moves. This is referred to as "time dilation." If you are standing on the top of Pike's Peak, time is moving faster for you than if you were standing at sea level.

relaxation. Jesus uses the yoke metaphor in the Gospel of Matthew where he is quoted as saying, "Take my yoke upon you, and learn from me; for I am gentle and lowly at heart, and you will find rest for your souls … for my yoke is easy and my burden is light" (Matt. 11:29, 30).

Two oxen yoked together walk beside each other helping with the same task. The book of Genesis uses the metaphor of *walking with God*, as it says in Genesis, chapter 6 verse 9, "Noah walked with God." The metaphor of being yoked to the Divine thus suggests the experience of oneness is not a static state or condition. Rather, it is an unfolding process with which we are "walking" cooperatively in step.

It was during my graduate school days while I was studying at Indiana University that I became deeply interested in meditation. I had been led to several books on yoga and had adopted a routine of practicing the asanas (postures), pranayama (breathing exercises) and meditation on a daily basis. One morning, after completing my routine of asanas and pranayama, I entered meditation and experienced the complete transcendent absorption referred to as *Samadhi* in the yogic literature. The spiritual life-energy had risen within me.* It was a profound experience of the isolation of the soul from my temporal body. I was consumed by intense bliss and the recognition that the awareness has an existence free from time and space, autonomous from my individuality. The "thousand-pedaled lotus," as it is described poetically in the yogic literature, had opened and blossomed within me.

At that time I concluded that this was the goal of the spiritual quest, to experientially know oneself essentially as existing in union with the eternal, Divine consciousness beyond the mind. I had

---

* This experience is perhaps the intended meaning of the obscure verse in the Gospel of John where it says: "Out of one's heart (lit. belly) shall flow rivers of living water" (John 7:38).

been spiritually awakened, liberated, at least for the moment, from temporality. I soon came to realize, however, that my experience was actually the beginning of a realization process that would continue to unfold as I moved through life. The oneness I had experienced would spontaneously begin to infuse and be integrated into my temporal life and action. Over time, I would come to know the beauty of motion within stillness, and stillness in motion.

Participating in the arts and in athletics is one means through which a person can appreciate oneness while physically active. Unity, in this context, means becoming one with your object of devotion or dedication while engaged in an activity. Artists seek to become one with their art; athletes seek to become one with their athletic event. The mystic seeks to become one with the Divine, to become one with that living infinite Ultimate Mystery many refer to as God. To become one with your object of devotion or dedication means not only to know it intimately, but also, to live in harmony with that endeavor. It is an unfolding process of perpetual becoming, a marriage, so to speak, that one lives in and grows with, not a static state of being.

When I play my musical instrument (the saxophone), I have played it for so long it has become a part of me. The saxophone now is an extension of myself. I can therefore lose myself, that is, my individuality, in the act of performance.

To learn something by heart is to make it a part of oneself, to become one with the process of living it, whether this is done through an art form or through learning how to apply a spiritual teaching. It implies spontaneity in its application, much like when we become fluent in speaking a second language. We experience a direct connection between impulse and action that no longer involves intellectual calculation.

Singularity as Cosmic Seed

The Upanishads conceive of the universe as existing in the beginning as a seed, within which all the laws and power of nature are
one, and which then begins to express itself as a living organism.[16]
From this perspective, the universe is not an object but a series of
events, a process that is perpetually and eternally unfolding from the
inner to the outer, from the micro to the macro level. The universe,
and God for that matter, is more of a verb than a noun.

My favorite symbol for oneness or unity, which captures this idea
of an unfolding process, is the *yin-yang*. Chinese Taoist philosophers
devised this symbol to depict complementary opposite values in
creation coexisting in a condition of harmony and mutual give-
and-take. People in Western cultures frequently ascribe good and
evil to the light and dark sides of this image, but such values are
not part of the Taoist interpretation. Rather, the yin or dark side
represents mystery, intuition, and the feminine principle, while the
yang or light portion symbolizes clarity, intellect, and the stereo-
typical masculine side of life. The large dots of opposing color in
each side of the symbol reveal that the complementary opposites
are inseparable and are forever interdependent. This prevents the
Taoist duality from being interpreted and applied simplistically.
According to the Tao Te Ching, one is to "keep the strength of a
man, but keep a woman's care"[17] A person must learn to balance the
yin and the yang, the masculine and the feminine within oneself,
and also, facilitate their complementary flow in creation.

Taoism teaches that multiplicity comes forth from oneness. As
it says in the Tao Te Ching, the "One begot two. Two begot three.
And three begot the 10,000 things,"[18] the number 10,000 being a
metaphor for unending variety.[19] Thus, "all is one" or Adviata is
fundamental to Taoist philosophy as well as to Indian philosophy.
In fact, oneness is found in the mystical traditions of each of the

great world religions where contemplative practice is emphasized. A mystic is a person who seeks union with the Divine through direct experience, and that experience is acquired through some form of contemplative spiritual practice. Not surprisingly, we can find evidence for oneness in modern-day science as well.

The yin-yang: symbol for complementary opposites in a condition of give-and-take, and existing in a state of oneness as represented by the enclosing circle

According to the big bang theory, in the beginning of the universe, all the matter in the universe was packed into a very small volume of infinite mass and density. Astrophysicists now refer to the universe prior to the Big Bang as a "singularity." This is described as a state of infinite gravity. Even time and space were compressed within this singularity.

When we see the Big Bang depicted on television or on a movie screen, we see a huge explosion of matter and light that fills up the empty space of the dark screen. But this animation is actually a misrepresentation of the primordial event. For in the beginning, there was no space to be filled, and for the first several million years after the initial event, scientists theorize that the universe was dark. The so-called Big Bang is now being described as an expansion or an unfolding of time and space, more like a balloon that is being inflated.

The idea that space-time expands as the universe unfolds raises the question: is the space-time continuum we experience merely a mental conception we construct to help us have some understanding of our universe? Or should space-time be thought of as an object, something that is "created" and has its own autonomous existence? If it is a mental conception, then space-time cannot exist independent of mind. Its reality requires a mind to conceive it. On the other hand, if it is an "object," created and expanding by virtue of the inflation of the universe, then we are left with a perplexing koan-like riddle asked by John Denker, author of the book entitled *The Quantum God*. If the universe is expanding like a balloon in which time and space only exist in the skin of the balloon, then Denker asks, "what is the balloon [i.e. space and time] expanding into?"[20] Such a koan brings us back to recognize what quantum mechanics as well as astrophysics has forced us to admit, that everything, including mind and matter, are interrelated and interdependent. One cannot exist without the other. We cannot get outside our awareness, our consciousness. The universe is expanding into the collective universal mind of which we are a part and a microcosm. The words of Carl Sagan again come to mind when he said: "We are a way the cosmos can know itself."[21]

As explained in Chapter 2, a wave behaves like a particle only when an interaction is being observed or recorded. Skeptics may say that a non-conscious observer can record the wave-particle collapse in quantum mechanics. However, if the recording of the event is deleted before being examined, then the waveform doesn't collapse. Thus, interaction that includes a conscious observer is necessary for the wave-particle collapse to occur. Without the presence of something that observes or records the interaction, quantum waves would not collapse to become particles.* Without consciousness, ideas do not form, take shape and become reality, and the primordial null-dimensional singularity, as incomprehensible and abstract as that concept is, would not have been conceivable. And what is a singularity but a condition where all is one. To borrow a metaphor from the Rig Veda, the singularity is analogous to *Hiranyagarbha*, the golden embryo or seed from which the unfolding process called the universe was born.[†22]

So it appears the ancient Indian and Taoist philosophers had it right long ago. Everything, be it time, space, mind, matter, energy, intelligence and consciousness, and life itself, came from that singularity or cosmic "seed." We have arrived at the same conclusion that the sages did some 2.5 millennia ago. It's just taken scientists 2500 years to catch up.

---

*   Some evolutionary biologists insist that consciousness is the result of complex biological processes, but this is only true for consciousness as exhibited by individual organisms. The "observer" interaction required for the collapse of waves into particles underlies the entire material universe. Biological evolution makes it possible for complex organisms to evolve so that the underlying universal consciousness can express itself.

†   The wave-particle collapse may serve as a way of understanding the relationship between spirit and soul. That is, when the spirit gains individual identity, it becomes a soul in a way analogous to when a wave of energy collapses and behaves as a particle.

Reviving Contemplative Practice

Listen deeply, I am quieter than silence.
Look deeply, I am closer than the I.
Dream deeply, and you will perceive my veil.
Sleep deeply, yet I remain awake.
Breathe deeply, and I will settle your mind.
Sing deeply, and you will know my heart.

Turn away from the senses so I can draw you near,
   absorb you into my Being.
Meditate deeply, and you will know me as
   a sightless newborn kitten knows
   its mother.
Drink deeply, and I will extinguish your thirst,
For I am wellspring and ocean, and the primal
   waters from which new creations are born.

Try to confine me and I will escape from
   my tomb.
Ascribe me a name and divisions will arise
   among you.
For I am the Lord beyond name and form,
The everlasting source of sound and light,
   of thought and breath,
Quieter than silence, closer than the I.

This poem, spoken through the voice of the universal Self, captures the inward turning of the mind during meditation, and brings us back to contemplative spirituality. It is through the regular exposure to the contemplative experience that the faculties of intuition, insight and realization are awakened, enabling us to appreciate the mystery of oneness. Through such an awakening we come to embrace the beauty of paradox and the reality of unity and diversity coexisting in a state of balance and mutual support. It is therefore vital that meditation becomes a daily practice in everyone's life, and that the education of young people includes contemplative experience.

So here are three things you can do to cultivate the experience of unity or oneness in your life.

1. Meditate every morning,
2. Meditate every evening,
3. Meditate in a group setting once a week to deepen your experience, receive guidance from a teacher, and reinforce regularity of practice.

During meditation, oneness is experienced as thoughts subside and the mind becomes absorbed in infinite awareness. This is where one experiences what in Indian philosophy is referred to as the "witness,"[23] which Henry David Thoreau in *Walden* refers to as the "spectator" (see chapter 2, page 47 for quote). A person enters what is described in the Mandukya Upanishad as the fourth state of consciousness, which is distinctly different from our experience in waking, dream and deep sleep.

> Beyond the senses, beyond the understanding, beyond all expression is The Fourth. It is pure unitary consciousness, wherein awareness of the world and of multiplicity is completely obliterated. It is ineffable peace. It is the supreme good. It is One without a second.[24]

Outside the contemplative experience, the blessing of oneness is experienced as wholeness, whereby one feels complete and fulfilled as a person, living in harmony with this on-going unfolding process called life. On this level, one perceives the universal truths that underlie the great religions.

All of the great religions, that is, Judaism, Hinduism, Christianity, Buddhism and Islam, embrace some form of the Golden Rule; with the exception of Taoism, each associates light with God, divinity or wisdom, and darkness with ignorance and losing one's way. Each emphasizes forgiveness and has some form of penitential practice or season; each encourages a form of reflective interior prayer or meditation; each teaches that a person should disengage the ego and act from a level free from self-centered interests, and each religion calls upon its followers to share their wealth to help people in need. These values and symbols are the threads that can unite humanity.

Meditation, as a regular daily practice, is imperative if we are going to enlarge our capacity to perceive the world in holistic ways, to "rewire" our "neural networks" as Leonard Susskind expresses it, so we can appreciate the space-time continuum and the quantum reality that underlies the experience of the material world. For when all is said and done, we must recognize that we are part of a cosmos that is a magnificent unfolding drama, a living illusion that is, to use the words of Carl Sagan, "the grandest of mysteries," a mystery so vast and deep, all we can do is marvel at its unlimited scope and surrender to it in reverent humility.

Mystery. If we look deeply enough, we find it to be the only Reality.

I began singing the moment
   creation breathed,
Whirling melodies
Set to the meters of heartbeats
   and quasars
Heard only when the ego sleeps.

I began singing before there
   was darkness,
While time still slumbered between
   the future and the past.
My drone is the first partial and
   the endless curve of space.

Come,
Sing with me.
Close your eyes and lips
   and follow my song
To its sacred source
Where sound and light dance
   together
Beneath the golden rays of knowing,
Trying their best to awaken you
   from history's dream.

APPENDIX 1

Meditation and the Gandharva Tradition

Meditation is an effective way to heighten mental clarity, alleviate stress, and achieve a tranquil state of quiet inner reflection. A technique derived from the Gandharva musical tradition in India allows practitioners to bring the harmony underlying creation to the surface of life where it can be experienced and lived in a practical way.

Think of the mind as a pond of water which, when left undisturbed, presents us with a clear picture of the images reflecting off its surface. It is the mind's nature to reflect what we take in through the senses, but tension and fatigue in daily life create "waves" on the surface of the mind, causing it to present us with a convoluted image, distorting our perception of reality.

Gandharva Meditation is a technique that enables us to restore the mind to its natural condition of tranquility so it can yield a truer reflection of reality. During Gandharva Meditation, the silence at the depths of the mind comes to the foreground of our experience while mental activity settles into the background and can even subside altogether. It is a psycho-physiological experience, simultaneously a condition of heightened awareness and deep relaxation. The technique does not involve forced concentration, and it is quite easy to learn. This form of meditation is not a mood, nor is it a form of self-hypnosis or autosuggestion. It is a state of consciousness as tangible and as real as waking, sleeping, or dreaming—a means of experiencing the ground of *being* that lies at the depths of our consciousness.

One first learns how to establish the proper conditions in the physiology for the body's metabolism to reduce significantly through the use of an ancient form of East Indian music. Then a technique is used that allows a person to cooperate with the mind's natural tendency to settle into the state of non-desire. This experience of inner pleasantness cultures in the individual the state of attunement characterized by a heightened state of cooperation between the voluntary and involuntary nervous systems. It is a procedure that is practiced twice a day and takes approximately twenty minutes.

For more information, contact:

Lifeworks Center
2417 West Jackson Street
Muncie, Indiana 47304
765-286-8221

Appendix 2

The Growth of Human Consciousness

The Nine Pivotal Awakenings

1. Awakening to "self-awareness"; approximate age: 0–1 year.
   Awareness of the difference between self and the object of perception.
2. Awakening to right and wrong, good and bad; approximate age: 1–2 years.
   Awareness of social rules and expectations.
3. Awakening to body as self; approximate age: 2–5 years.
   Awareness of embarrassment and being naked, awareness of death.
4. Awakening of the intellect; approximate age: 5–12 years.
   Increased ability to think logically.
5. Puberty and the awakening of sexuality; approximate age: 12–18 years.
   Awareness of sexual differences and the desire for intimacy. One becomes motivated by physical needs and the needs of the ego
6. Awakening to the higher spiritual "Self"; approximate age: 18–25 years.
   Awareness of an identity independent of physical self and ego. Recognition of moral dilemmas and imperfection as part of the human condition.

7. Awareness of the higher "Self" permanently established; approximate age: 25–35 years.
   Actions become motivated by the needs of the environment, the needs of others and the "greater good." The higher Self is recognized as eternal, conquering the fear of death.
8. Awareness of subtle values revealed through ongoing realizations; approximate age: 35–50 years.
   Perceiving life and meaning in terms of symbolism, metaphor, and myth. One is now increasingly able to follow one's "inner light."
9. Awakening to "oneness" and the interconnectedness of all things; approximate age: 50 years and older.
   Realization that the higher Self is the "Self of all beings." Experiencing both the joy and pain of others as one's own.

Cross-cultural metaphors for awakening:
   Caterpillar becoming a butterfly
   Second birth.

Endnotes

Preface

1   Susskind, Leonard. *The Black Hole War; My Battle with Stephen Hawking to Make the World Safe for Quantum Mechanics.* New York: Little, Brown and Co., 2008, pp. 5, 6.

Chapter 1

1   Sagan, Carl; Druyan, Ann & Soter, Steven. *Cosmos.* 1980, Episode 1.

2   Keating, Thomas. *Seekers of Ultimate Mystery.* Contemplative Outreach News (www.contemplativeoutreach.org): Vol. 25, no. 2, June 2010.

3   Rohr, Richard. *The Naked Now.* New York: Crossroads Publishing, 2009, p. 146.

4   Ibid., pp. 144–145.

5   Feng, Gia-Fu, and English, Jane. *Tao Te Ching.* 25th Anniversary Edition. New York: Vintage Books, 1997, Chapter 22.

6   Prabavananda, S. and Manchester, F. *The Upanishads: Breath of the Eternal.* New York: The New American Library, 1948, p. 4.

7   Rohr, Richard. *The Naked Now.* New York: Crossroads Publishing, 2009, p. 146.

8   Keating, Thomas. *Seekers of Ultimate Mystery.* Contemplative Outreach News (www.contemplativeoutreach.org): Vol. 25, no. 2, June 2010.

9   Dossey, Larry. *Space, Time and Medicine.* Boulder and London: Shambhala Publications, 1982, pp. 233–234.

10 Prabavananda, S. and Manchester, F. *The Upanishads: Breath of the Eternal*. New York: The New American Library, 1948, pp. 30, 31.

Chapter 2

1   O'Flathery, Wendy D. (trans). *The Rig Veda: An Anthology.* London: Penguin Books, 1981, p. 122.
2   Feng, Gia-Fu, and English, Jane. *Tao Te Ching.* 25th Anniversary Edition. New York: Vintage Books, 1997, Chapter 28.
3   Nikhilananda, Swami. *The Upanishads: Katha, Isa, Kena, and Mundaka,* Vol. 2. New York: Ramakrishna-Vivekananda Center, 1949, p. 236.
4   Hanh, Thich Nhat. *Living Buddha, Living Christ.* New York: Riverhead Books, 1995, p. 10.
5   Merton, Thomas. *Spiritual Direction and Meditation.* Collegeville, Minnesota: Order of St. Benedict, 1960, pp. 52–54.
6   Thoreau. *Walden,* with an introduction and annotations by Bill McKribben, 127–128.
7   Müller, Max. *The Dhammapada,* Ch. 21: verses 296–301, p. 80.
8   Prabavananda, S. and Manchester, F. *The Upanishads: Breath of the Eternal*. New York: The New American Library, 1948, p. 20.
9   Chuang Tzu (trans. Watson). *The Complete Works of Chuang Tzu.* New York: Columbia University Press: 1968, p. 48.
10 Selye, H. *From Dream to Discovery: On Being a Scientist.* New York: McGraw-Hill, 1964, p. 47.
11 Ibid., p. 47.
12 Ibid., p. 48.

13 Susskind, Leonard. *The Black Hole War; My Battle with Stephen Hawking to Make the World Safe for Quantum Mechanics.* New York: Little, Brown and Co. 2008, p. 422.
14 Ibid., p. 300.
15 Jeans, James Hopwood. *The Mysterious Universe.* Cambridge: Cambridge University Press, 1930.
16 Ibid., pp. 437–438.
17 Rumi (trans. Helminski). *The Rumi Collection.* Boston: Shambala Classics, 2000, p. 32.
18 Sagan, Carl. *The Demon-Haunted World: Science as a Candle in the Dark.* New York: Ballantine Books. 1997.
19 https://www.goodreads.com/author/quotes/821936.Niels_ Bohr.
20 Susskind, Leonard. The Black Hole War; My Battle with Stephen Hawking to Make the World Safe for Quantum Mechanics. New York: Little, Brown and Co. 2008, p. 435.

Chapter 3

1 O'Flathery, Wendy D. (trans). *The Rig Veda: An Anthology.* London: Penguin Books, 1981, p. 32.
2 Rohr, Richard. *Falling Upward: A Spirituality for the Two Halves of Life.* San Francisco: Jossey Bass, 2011.
3 Spong, John S. *Public Lecture.* Chautauqua Institution, June 29, 2010.
4 Bronowsky, Jacob. The ascent of Man. Boston/Toronto: Little, Brown and Co., 1973, pp. 1–2.
5 Letterman, David. Interview with Oprah Winfrey. Ball State University. (http://www.youtube.com/watch?v=Xry51JBMj4w): Nov. 26, 2012.

Chapter 4

1   Davies, A. Powell. *The First Christian: A study of St. Paul and Christian Origins.* New York: Farrar, Straus and Cudahy, 1957, p. 131.

2   Ibid., p. 131.

3   Ibid., pp. 135, 136.

4   O'Flathery, Wendy D. (trans). *The Rig Veda: An Anthology.* London: Penguin Books, 1981, p. 124

5   Ibid., p. 122.

6   Ibid., p. 122.

7   Ibid., pp. 129, 130.

8   Ibid., pp. 128, 190–191.

9   Ibid., p. 121.

10 Ibid., p. 128.

11 Ibid., p. 122.

12 Ibid., p. 121.

13 Allegro, John. *The Dead Sea Scrolls and the Christian Myth.* Buffalo, NY.: Prometheus Books, 1984, p. 174.

14 Ibid., pp. 96–97.

15 Davies, A. Powell. *The First Christian: A study of St. Paul and Christian Origins.* NewYork: Farrar, Straus and Cudahy, 1957, pp. 120–121.

16 Ibid, pp. 119–124.

17 O'Flathery, Wendy D. *The Rig Veda: An Anthology.* London: Penguin Books, 1981, pp. 30–31.

18 Ibid., p. 32.

Chapter 5

1 See *The Astronomical Significance of Stonehenge* by Carl Newham, Wales: Moon Publications, 1972.

2 Harshananda, S. *All About Hindu Temples.* Madras: Sri Ramakrishna Math Press, 1992, p. 2.

3 Prabavananda, S. and Manchester, F. *The Upanishads: Breath of the Eternal.* New York: The New American Library, 1948, p. 79.

4 Deutsch, Eliot (trans.) *The Bhagavad Gita* (Ch. X:11). New York: Holt, Rinehart and Winston, 1968, p. 89.

5 Harshananda, S. *All About Hindu Temples.* Madras: Sri Ramakrishna Math Press, 1992, p. 13.

6 Shanley, L. ed. *Henry David Thoreau, The Illustrated Walden.* Princeton: Princeton University Press, p. 321.

7 Nikhilananda, Swami. *The Upanishads: Katha, Isa, Kena, and Mundaka,* Vol. I. New York: Ramakrishna-Vivekananda Center, 1949, p. 5.

8 Ibid., p. 13

9 Shapiro, Rami. *Hasidic Tales.* Woodstock, Vermont: Skylight Paths Publishing, 2005, p. ix.

10 Cross, St. John of the. *Living Flame of Love.* New York: Image Books, 1962, p. 33.

11 Rajagopalachari, C. *Mahabharata.* Bombay: Bharatiya Vidya Bhavan, 1990, pp. 137–138.

12 Prabavananda, S. and Manchester, F. *The Upanishads: Breath of the Eternal.* New York: The New American Library, 1948, p. 65.

13 Ruhala, W. *What the Buddha Taught.* New York: Grove Press,1959, pp. 35–43.

Chapter 6

1   Thoreau, H. D. *A Week on the Concord Merrimack Rivers.*
    New York: Thomas Y. Crowell Co., 1966, p. 213.
2   Emerson, R.W. *The Complete Essays and Other Writings
    of Ralph Waldo Emerson*, ed. Brooks Atkinson. New York:
    Random House, 1940, p. 264.
3   Ibid., p. 262.
4   Prabavananda, S. and Manchester, F. *The Upanishads: Breath
    of the Eternal.* New York: The New American Library, 1948,
    p. 43.
5   Deutsch, Eliot (trans.) *The Bhagavad Gita* (Ch. IX:29). New
    York: Holt, Rinehart and Winston, 1968, p. 86.
6   Prabavananda, S. and Manchester, F. *The Upanishads: Breath
    of the Eternal.* New York: The New American Library, 1948,
    p. 24.
7   Ibid., p. 21.
8   Dossey, Larry. *Space, Time and Medicine.* Boulder: Shambala,
    1982, pp. 102–107.
9   Susskind, Leonard. *The Black Hole War; My Battle with
    Stephen Hawking to Make the World Safe for Quantum
    Mechanics.* New York: Little, Brown and Co., 2008, p. 298
10 Ibid., p. 434.
11 Prabavananda, S. and Manchester, F. *The Upanishads: Breath
    of the Eternal.* New York: The New American Library, 1948,
    p. 68.
12 Capra, Fritjof. *The Tao of Physics.* Boulder: Shambala, 1983,
    pp. 183, 184.
13 Deutsch, Eliot (trans.) *The Bhagavad Gita* (Ch. IV:20). New
    York: Holt, Rinehart and Winston, 1968, p. 56.
14 Ibid., p. 57.
15 Ibid., p. 6.

16 Prabavananda, S. and Manchester, F. *The Upanishads: Breath of the Eternal*. New York: The New American Library, 1948, p. 80.

17 Feng, Gia-Fu, and English, Jane. *Tao Te Ching*. 25th Anniversary Edition. New York: Vintage Books, 1997, Chapter 28.

18 Feng, Gia-Fu, and English, Jane. *Tao Te Ching*. 25th Anniversary Edition. New York: Vintage Books, 1997, Chapter 42.

19 Ibid., ch. 25.

20 Denker, John. *The Quantum God (Why Our Grandchildren Won't Know Atheism)*. Bloomington, IN: iUniverse Books, 2010.

21 Sagan, Carl; Druyan, Ann & Soter, Steven. *Cosmos*. 1980, Episode 1.

22 O'Flathery, Wendy D. *The Rig Veda: An Anthology*. London: Penguin Books, 1981, p. 27.

23 Deutsch, Eliot (trans.) *The Bhagavad Gita* (Ch. XIII:22). New York: Holt, Rinehart and Winston, 1968, p. 110.

24 Prabavananda, S. and Manchester, F. *The Upanishads: Breath of the Eternal*. New York: The New American Library, 1948, pp. 50–51.

About the Author

George Wolfe is Professor Emeritus at Ball State University where he served as director of the Center for Peace and Conflict Studies from 2002 to 2006, and Coordinator of Outreach Programs from 2007 to 2014. He is a certified mediator and was trained to conduct interfaith dialogue at All-Faiths Seminary International in New York City where he was ordained an interfaith minister. In 1991, he was awarded an open fellowship from the Eli Lilly Endowment which made possible his first trip to India where he became interested in the nonviolent philosophy of Mahatma Gandhi.

Wolfe received his doctorate in higher education administration from Indiana University. As an educator, he has lectured both within and outside the United States on topics related to nonviolence, peace education, academic freedom, and the role of the arts in social activism. He has been a featured speaker in the Hall of Philosophy at Chautauqua Institution and has served as a panelist at the annual International Conference on World Affairs in Boulder, Colorado. He has also served on the advisory council of the Toda Institute for Peace, Policy and Global Research, and served as a visiting scholar at Limburg Catholic University in Hasselt, Belgium. In the spring of

2007, he presented peace education workshops in the island nation of Saint Lucia by invitation of the Ministry of Education.

Dr. Wolfe is also a classical saxophonist who held the rank of Professor of Music Performance at Ball State University. He has appeared as a soloist with such ensembles as the Royal Band of the Belgian Air Force, Chautauqua Motet Choir, the U.S. Navy Band Brass Quintet, the Indianapolis Children's Choir and the Saskatoon Symphony. He has also given recitals and master classes throughout the United States, as well as at major conservatories and universities in Europe, Central America, and the Far East.

Index

W

Y

Z

Dignity Press
World Dignity University Press

Selected Books

For more details about these books, for a complete catalog of
Dignity Press books and for information about Dignity Press,
please consult www.dignitypress.org

Michael H. Prosser, Mansoureh Shanifzadeh, and Shengyong Zhang
Finding Cross-Cultural Common Ground

March 2013
511 pages, paperback
ISBN 978-1-937570-25-5

Howard Richards and Joanna Swanger
Gandhi and the Future of Economics

Edited by Ivo Coelho
March 2013
306 pages, paperback
ISBN 978-1-937570-29-3

Hilarie Roseman

Generating Forgiveness and Constructing Peace through Truthful Dialogue: Abrahamic Perspectives

May 2014
432 pages, paperback
ISBN 978-1-937570-48-4

David Y.F. Ho

Enlightened or Mad?

A Psychoanalyst Glimpses into Mystical Magnanimity
October 2014
354 pages, paperback
ISBN 978-1-937570-51-4

Mark Tarver

Conversations of Taoist Master Fu Hsiang

December 2014
ca. 120 pages, paperback
ISBN 978-1-937570-52-1

Kathy Beckwith

A Mighty Case against War

December 2014
ca. 360 pages, paperback
ISBN 978-1-937570-32-3

CPSIA information can be obtained
at www.ICGtesting.com
Printed in the USA
FFOW04n0940160215
11070FF